The
Oxford
Book of
Christmas
Poems

The
Oxford
Book of
Christmas
Poems

Edited by Michael Harrison
and Christopher Stuart-Clark

OXFORD
UNIVERSITY PRESS

OXFORD
UNIVERSITY PRESS

Great Clarendon Street, Oxford OX2 6DP

Oxford University Press is a department of the University of Oxford.
It furthers the University's objective of excellence in research, scholarship,
and education by publishing worldwide in

Oxford   New York

Auckland   Cape Town   Dar es Salaam   Hong Kong   Karachi
Kuala Lumpur   Madrid   Melbourne   Mexico City   Nairobi
New Delhi   Shanghai   Taipei   Toronto

With offices in

Argentina   Austria   Brazil   Chile   Czech Republic   France   Greece
Guatemala   Hungary   Italy   Japan   Poland   Portugal   Singapore
South Korea   Switzerland   Thailand   Turkey   Ukraine   Vietnam

Oxford is a registered trade mark of Oxford University Press
in the UK and in certain other countries

First published 1983
This paperback edition 2005

British Library Cataloguing in Publication Data

Data available

Cover illustration by Jane Ray

Contents

'The sky turns dark, the year grows old . . .'

'This was the moment when Before Turned into After . . .'

'Glad Christmas comes, and every hearth Makes room to bid him welcome now . . .'

'Open you the East door
And let the New Year in.'

The sky turns dark,
the year grows old . . .

The Coming of the Cold

The ribs of leaves lie in the dust,
The beak of frost has pecked the bough,
The briar bears its thorn, and drought
Has left its ravage on the field.
The season's wreckage lies about,
Late autumn fruit is rotted now.
All shade is lean, the antic branch
Jerks skyward at the touch of wind,
Dense trees no longer hold the light,
The hedge and orchard grove are thinned.
The dank bark dries beneath the sun,
The last of harvesting is done.

All things are brought to barn and fold.
The oak leaves strain to be unbound,
The sky turns dark, the year grows old,
The buds draw in before the cold.

The small brook dies within its bed;
The stem that holds the bee is prone;
Old hedgerows keep the leaves; the phlox,
That late autumnal bloom, is dead.

All summer green is now undone:
The hills are grey, the trees are bare,
The mould upon the branch is dry,
The fields are harsh and bare, the rocks
Gleam sharply on the narrow sight.
The land is desolate, the sun
No longer gilds the scene at noon;
Winds gather in the north and blow
Bleak clouds across the heavy sky,
And frost is marrow-cold, and soon
Winds bring a fine and bitter snow.

Theodore Roethke

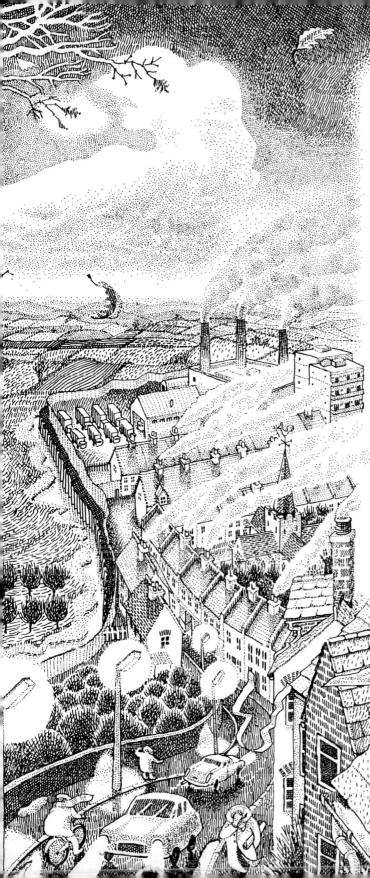

Winter Days

Biting air
Winds blow
City streets
Under snow

Noses red
Lips sore
Runny eyes
Hands raw

Chimneys smoke
Cars crawl
Piled snow
On garden wall

Slush in gutters
Ice in lanes
Frosty patterns
On window panes

Morning call
Lift up head
Nipped by winter
Stay in bed

Gareth Owen

Sleet

The first snow was sleet. It swished heavily
Out of a cloud black enough to hold snow.
It was fine in the wind, but couldn't bear to touch
Anything solid. It died a pauper's death.

Now snow – it grins like a maniac in the moon.
It puts a glove on your face. It stops gaps.
It catches your eye and your breath. It settles down
Ponderously crushing trees with its airy ounces.

But today it was sleet, dissolving spiders on cheekbones,
Being melting spit on the glass, smudging the mind
That humped itself by the fire, turning away
From the ill wind, the sky filthily weeping.

Norman MacCaig

Snowflakes

And did you know
That every flake of snow
That forms so high
In the grey winter sky
And falls so far,
Is a bright six-pointed star?
Each crystal grows
A flower as perfect as a rose.
Lace could never make
The patterns of a flake.
No brooch
Of figured silver could approach
Its delicate craftsmanship. And think:
Each pattern is distinct.
Of all the snowflakes floating there –
The million million in the air –
None is the same. Each star
Is newly forged, as faces are,
Shaped to its own design
Like yours and mine.
And yet . . . each one
Melts when its flight is done;
Holds frozen loveliness
A moment, even less;
Suspends itself in time –
And passes like a rhyme.

Clive Sansom

Snow-Bound

Shut in from all the world without,
We sat the clean-winged hearth about,
Content to let the north-wind roar
In baffled rage at pane and door,
While the red logs before us beat
The frost-line back with tropic heat;
And ever, when a louder blast
Shook beam and rafter as it passed,
The merrier up its roaring draught
The great throat of the chimney laughed.

John Greenleaf Whittier

Safe

Come, stir the fire,
The lamps unlit
Leave, while we sit
Close to the glow,
And fire and shadow flit
About the room, and fight
For love of it.

Cold winds blow
Whirling in the drear
Night outside; the blaze
Uncoils its tentacles, and here
We in a dream-daze
With the lamps unlit,
Safe in firelight sit.

James Walker

December

While snows the window-panes bedim,
 The fire curls up a sunny charm,
Where, creaming o'er the pitcher's rim,
 The flowering ale is set to warm;
Mirth, full of joy as summer bees,
 Sits there, its pleasures to impart,
And children, 'tween their parents' knees,
 Sing scraps of carols o'er by heart.

And some, to view the winter weathers,
 Climb up the window-seat with glee,
Likening the snow to falling feathers,
 In fancy's infant ecstasy;
Laughing, with superstitious love,
 O'er visions wild that youth supplies,
Of people pulling geese above,
 And keeping Christmas in the skies.

As tho' the homestead trees were drest,
 In lieu of snow, with dancing leaves,
As tho' the sun-dried martin's nest,
 Instead of ickles, hung the eaves,
The children hail the happy day –
 As if the snow were April's grass,
And pleas'd, as 'neath the warmth of May,
 Sport o'er the water froze to glass.

John Clare

Advent: A Carol

What did you hear?
  Said stone to echo:
All that you told me,
  Said echo to stone.

Tidings, said echo,
  Tidings, said stone,
Tidings of wonder
  Said echo to stone.

Who then shall hear them?
  Said stone to echo:
All people on earth,
  Said echo to stone.

Turned into one,
  Echo and stone,
The word for all coming
  Turned into one.

Patric Dickinson

December
Prayer to St Nicholas

Patron of all those who do good by stealth –
Slipping three bags of gold in through the window
To save three desperate girls, restoring
Dead boys to life out of the pickling tub
Of an Anatolian Sweeney Todd –
Teach us to give with simplicity, and not with an eye
To the main chance: it's less than
Three weeks' shopping time to Christmas.

John Heath-Stubbs

Advent 1955

The Advent wind begins to stir
With sea-like sounds in our Scotch fir,
It's dark at breakfast, dark at tea,
And in between we only see
Clouds hurrying across the sky
And rain-wet roads the wind blows dry
And branches bending to the gale
Against great skies all silver-pale.
The world seems travelling into space,
And travelling at a faster pace
Than in the leisured summer weather
When we and it sit out together,
For now we feel the world spin round
On some momentous journey bound –
Journey to what? to whom? to where?
The Advent bells call out 'Prepare,
Your world is journeying to the birth
Of God made Man for us on earth.'

And how, in fact, do we prepare
For the great day that waits us there –
The twenty-fifth day of December,
The birth of Christ? For some it means
An interchange of hunting scenes
On coloured cards. And I remember
Last year I sent out twenty yards,
Laid end to end, of Christmas cards
To people that I scarcely know –
They'd sent a card to me, and so
I had to send one back. Oh dear!
Is this a form of Christmas cheer?
Or is it, which is less surprising,
My pride gone in for advertising?
The only cards that really count
Are that extremely small amount
From real friends who keep in touch
And are not rich but love us much.
Some ways indeed are very odd
By which we hail the birth of God.

We raise the price of things in shops,
We give plain boxes fancy tops
And lines which traders cannot sell
Thus parcell'd go extremely well.
We dole out bribes we call a present
To those to whom we must be pleasant
For business reasons. Our defence is
These bribes are charged against expenses
And bring relief in Income Tax.
Enough of these unworthy cracks!
'The time draws near the birth of Christ',
A present that cannot be priced
Given two thousand years ago.
Yet if God had not given so
He still would be a distant stranger
And not the Baby in the manger.

John Betjeman

This was the moment when Before
Turned into After . . .

Christmas Morn

Shall I tell you what will come
to Bethlehem on Christmas morn,
who will kneel them gently down
before the Lord new-born?

One small fish from the river,
with scales of red, red gold,
one wild bee from the heather,
one grey lamb from the fold,
one ox from the high pasture,
one black bull from the herd,
one goatling from the far hills,
one white, white bird.

And many children – God give them grace,
bringing tall candles to light Mary's face.

Ruth Sawyer

Joseph was an Old Man

Joseph was an old man,
    and an old man was he,
When he wedded Mary,
    in the land of Galilee.

Joseph and Mary walked
    through the orchard good,
Where was cherries and berries,
    so red as any blood.

Joseph and Mary walked
    through an orchard green,
Where was berries and cherries,
    as thick as might be seen.

O then bespoke Mary,
   so meek and so mild:
'Pluck me one cherry, Joseph,
   for I am with child.'

O then bespoke Joseph,
   with words most unkind:
'Let him pluck thee a cherry
   that brought thee with child.'

O then bespoke the babe
   within his mother's womb:
'Bow down then the tallest tree,
   for my mother to have some.'

Then bowed down the highest tree
   unto his mother's hand;
Then she cried, 'See, Joseph,
   I have cherries at command.'

O then bespoke Joseph:
   'I have done Mary wrong;
But cheer up, my dearest,
   and be not cast down.'

Then Mary plucked a cherry,
   as red as the blood,
Then Mary went home
   with her heavy load.

Then Mary took her babe,
   and sat him on her knee,
Saying, 'My dear son, tell me,
   what this world will be.'

'O I shall be as dead, mother,
    as the stones in the wall;
O the stones in the streets, mother,
    shall mourn for me all.

'Upon Easter day, mother,
    my uprising shall be;
O the sun and the moon, mother,
    shall both rise with me.'

Unknown

In the Town

JOSEPH   Take heart, the journey's ended:
    I see the twinkling lights,
Where we shall be befriended
    On this the night of nights.

MARY   Now praise the Lord that led us
    So safe into the town,
Where men will feed and bed us,
    And I can lay me down.

JOSEPH   And how then shall we praise him?
    Alas, my heart is sore
That we no gifts can raise him,
    We are so very poor.

MARY   We have as much as any
    That on the earth do live,
Although we have no penny,
    We have ourselves to give.

JOSEPH   Look yonder, wife, look yonder!
    A hostelry I see,
Where travellers that wander
    Will very welcome be.

MARY The house is tall and stately,
    The door stands open thus;
Yet husband, I fear greatly
    That inn is not for us.

JOSEPH God save you, gentle master!
    Your littlest room indeed
With plainest walls of plaster
    Tonight will serve our need.

HOST For lordlings and for ladies
    I've lodgings and to spare;
For you and yonder maid is
    No closet anywhere.

JOSEPH Take heart, take heart, sweet Mary,
    Another inn I spy,
Whose host will not be chary
    To let us easy lie.

MARY O aid me, I am ailing,
    My strength is nearly gone;
I feel my limbs are failing,
    And yet we must go on.

JOSEPH God save you, Hostess, kindly!
    I pray you, house my wife,
Who bears beside me blindly
    The burden of her life.

HOSTESS My guests are rich men's daughters,
    And sons, I'd have you know!
Seek out the poorer quarters,
    Where ragged people go.

JOSEPH Good sir, my wife's in labour,
    Some corner let us keep.

HOST Not I: knock up my neighbour,
    And as for me, I'll sleep.

MARY   In all the lighted city
       Where rich men welcome win,
   Will not one house for pity
       Take two poor strangers in?

JOSEPH   Good woman, I implore you,
       Afford my wife a bed.

HOSTESS   Nay, nay, I've nothing for you
       Except the cattle shed.

MARY   Then gladly in the manger
       Our bodies we will house,
   Since men tonight are stranger
       Than asses are and cows.

JOSEPH   Take heart, take heart, sweet Mary,
       The cattle are our friends,
   Lie down, lie down, sweet Mary,
       For here our journey ends.

MARY   Now praise the Lord that found me
       This shelter in the town,
   Where I with friends around me
       May lay my burden down.

Unknown

Minstrel's Song

I've just had an astounding dream as I lay in the straw.
I dreamed a star fell on to the straw beside me
And lay blazing. Then when I looked up
I saw a bull come flying through a sky of fire
And on its shoulders a huge silver woman
Holding the moon. And afterwards there came
A donkey flying through that same burning heaven
And on its shoulders a colossal man
Holding the sun. Suddenly I awoke
And saw a bull and a donkey kneeling in the straw,
And the great moving shadows of a man and a woman –
I say they were a man and a woman but
I dare not say what I think they were. I did not dare to look.
I ran out here into the freezing world
Because I dared not look. Inside that shed.

A star is coming this way along the road.
If I were not standing upright, this would be a dream.
A star the shape of a sword of fire, point-downward,
Is floating along the road. And now it rises.
It is shaking fire on to the roofs and the gardens.
And now it rises above the animal shed
Where I slept till the dream woke me. And now
The star is standing over the animal shed.

Ted Hughes

The Innkeeper's Wife

I love this byre. Shadows are kindly here.
The light is flecked with travelling stars of dust.
So quiet it seems after the inn-clamour,
Scraping of fiddles and the stamping feet.
Only the cows, each in her patient box,
Turn their slow eyes, as we and the sunlight enter,
Their slowly rhythmic mouths.
                      'That is the stall,
Carpenter. You see it's too far gone
For patching or repatching. My husband made it,
And he's been gone these dozen years and more . . .'
Strange how this lifeless thing, degraded wood
Split from the tree and nailed and crucified
To make a wall, outlives the mastering hand
That struck it down, the warm firm hand
That touched my body with its wandering love.
'No let the fire take them. Strip every board
And make a new beginning. Too many memories lurk
Like worms in this old wood. That piece you're holding –
That patch of grain with the giant's thumbprint –
I stared at it a full hour when he died:
Its grooves are down my mind. And that board there
Baring its knot-hole like a missing jig-saw –
I remember another hand along its rim.
No, not my husband's, and why I should remember
I cannot say. It was a night in winter.
Our house was full, tight-packed as salted herrings –

So full, they said, we had to hold our breaths
To close the door and shut the night-air out!
And then two travellers came. They stood outside
Across the threshold, half in the ring of light
And half beyond it. I would have let them in
Despite the crowding – the woman was past her time –
But I'd no mind to argue with my husband,
The flagon in my hand and half the inn
Still clamouring for wine. But when trade slackened,
And all our guests had sung themselves to bed
Or told the floor their troubles, I came out here
Where he had lodged them. The man was standing
As you are now, his hand smoothing that board. –
He was a carpenter, I heard them say.
She rested on the straw, and on her arm
A child was lying. None of your creased-faced brats
Squalling their lungs out. Just lying there
As calm as a new-dropped calf – his eyes wide open,
And gazing round as if the world he saw
In the chaff-strewn light of the stable lantern
Was something beautiful and new and strange.
Ah well, he'll have learnt different now, I reckon,
Wherever he is. And why I should recall
A scene like that, when times I would remember
Have passed beyond reliving, I cannot think.
It's a trick you're served by old possessions:
They have their memories too – too many memories.
Well, I must go in. There are meals to serve.
Join us there, Carpenter, when you've had enough
Of cattle-company. The world is a sad place,
But wine and music blunt the truth of it.'

Clive Sansom

Christmas Landscape

Tonight the wind gnaws
with teeth of glass,
the jackdaw shivers
in caged branches of iron,
the stars have talons.

There is hunger in the mouth
of vole and badger,
silver agonies of breath
in the nostril of the fox,
ice on the rabbit's paw.

Tonight has no moon,
no food for the pilgrim;
the fruit tree is bare,
the rose bush a thorn
and the ground is bitter with stones.

But the mole sleeps, and the hedgehog
lies curled in a womb of leaves,
the bean and the wheat-seed
hug their germs in the earth
and the stream moves under the ice.

Tonight there is no moon,
but a new star opens
like a silver trumpet over the dead.
Tonight in a nest of ruins
the blessèd babe is laid.

And the fir tree warms to a bloom of candles,
the child lights his lantern,
stares at his tinselled toy;
our hearts and hearths
smoulder with live ashes.

In the blood of our grief
the cold earth is suckled,
in our agony the womb
convulses its seed,
in the cry of anguish
the child's first breath is born.

Laurie Lee

BC : AD

This was the moment when Before
Turned into After, and the future's
Uninvented timekeepers presented arms.

This was the moment when nothing
Happened. Only dull peace
Sprawled boringly over the earth.

This was the moment when even energetic Romans
Could find nothing better to do
Than counting heads in remote provinces.

And this was the moment
When a few farm workers and three
Members of an obscure Persian sect

Walked haphazard by starlight straight
Into the kingdom of heaven.

U. A. Fanthorpe

O Simplicitas

An angel came to me
And I was unprepared
To be what God was using.
Mother I was to be.
A moment I despaired,
Thought briefly of refusing.
The angel knew I heard.
According to God's Word
I bowed to this strange choosing.

A palace should have been
The birthplace of a king
(I had no way of knowing).
We went to Bethlehem;
It was so strange a thing.
The wind was cold, and blowing,
My cloak was old, and thin.
They turned us from the inn;
The town was overflowing.

God's Word, a child so small,
Who still must learn to speak,
Lay in humiliation.
Joseph stood, strong and tall.
The beasts were warm and meek
And moved with hesitation.
The Child born in a stall?
I understood it: all.
Kings came in adoration.

Perhaps it was absurd:
The stable set apart,
The sleepy cattle lowing;
And the incarnate Word
Resting against my heart.
My joy was overflowing.
The shepherds came, adored
The folly of the Lord,
Wiser than all men's knowing.

Madeleine L'Engle

Carol

Mary laid her Child among
　　The bracken-fronds of night –
And by the glimmer round His head
　　All the barn was lit.

Mary held her Child above
　　The miry, frozen farm –
And by the fire within His limbs
　　The resting roots were warm.

Mary hid her Child between
　　Hillocks of hard sand –
By singing water in His veins
　　Grass sprang from the ground.

Mary nursed her Child beside
　　The gardens of a grave –
And by the death within His bones
　　The dead became alive.

Norman Nicholson

The Mother's Song

It is so still in the house.
There is a calm in the house;
The snowstorm wails out there,
And the dogs are rolled up with snouts under the tail.
My little boy is sleeping on the ledge,
On his back he lies, breathing through his open mouth.
His little stomach is bulging round –
Is it strange if I start to cry with joy?

Eskimo
Translated by Peter Freuchen

A Cradle Song

Sweet dreams, form a shade
O'er my lovely infant's head;
Sweet dreams of pleasant streams
By happy, silent, moony beams.

Sweet sleep, with soft down
Weave thy brows an infant crown.
Sweet sleep, Angel mild,
Hover o'er my happy child.

Sweet smiles, in the night
Hover over my delight;
Sweet smiles, mother's smiles,
All the livelong night beguiles.

Sweet moans, dovelike sighs,
Chase not slumber from thy eyes.
Sweet moans, sweeter smiles,
All the dovelike moans beguiles.

Sleep, sleep, happy child,
All creation slept and smil'd;
Sleep, sleep, happy sleep,
While o'er thee thy mother weep.

Sweet babe, in thy face
Holy image I can trace.
Sweet babe once like thee,
Thy Maker lay and wept for me,

Wept for me, for thee, for all,
When He was an infant small.
Thou His image ever see,
Heavenly face that smiles on thee,

Smiles on thee, on me, on all;
Who became an infant small.
Infant smiles are His own smiles;
Heaven and earth to peace beguiles.

William Blake

Mary's Song

Sleep, King Jesus,
Your royal bed
Is made of hay
In a cattle-shed.
Sleep, King Jesus,
Do not fear,
Joseph is watching
And waiting near.

Warm in the wintry air
You lie,
The ox and the donkey
Standing by,
With summer eyes
They seem to say:
Welcome, Jesus,
On Christmas Day!

Sleep, King Jesus:
Your diamond crown
High in the sky
Where the stars look down.
Let your reign
Of love begin,
That all the world
May enter in.

Charles Causley

A Christmas Hymn

*And some of the Pharisees from
among the multitude said unto him,
Master, rebuke thy disciples.*

*And he answered and said unto
them, I tell you that, if these should
hold their peace, the stones would
immediately cry out.*

ST. LUKE XIX, 39–40

A stable-lamp is lighted
Whose glow shall wake the sky;
The stars shall bend their voices,
And every stone shall cry.
And every stone shall cry,
And straw like gold shall shine;
A barn shall harbour heaven,
A stall become a shrine.

This child through David's city
Shall ride in triumph by;
The palm shall strew its branches,
And every stone shall cry.
And every stone shall cry,
Though heavy, dull and dumb,
And lie within the roadway
To pave his kingdom come.

Yet he shall be forsaken,
And yielded up to die;
The sky shall groan and darken,
And every stone shall cry.
And every stone shall cry,
For stony hearts of men:
God's blood upon the spearhead,
God's love refused again.

But now, as at the ending,
The low is lifted high;
The stars shall bend their voices,
And every stone shall cry.
And every stone shall cry,
In praises of the child
By whose descent among us
The worlds are reconciled.

Richard Wilbur

A Christmas Carol

The Christ-child lay on Mary's lap,
    His hair was like a light.
(O weary, weary were the world,
    But here is all aright.)

The Christ-child lay on Mary's breast,
    His hair was like a star.
(O stern and cunning are the kings,
    But here the true hearts are.)

The Christ-child lay on Mary's heart,
    His hair was like a fire.
(O weary, weary is the world,
    But here the world's desire.)

The Christ-child stood at Mary's knee,
    His hair was like a crown,
And all the flowers looked up at him,
    And all the stars looked down.

G. K. Chesterton

'I saw a Stable'

I saw a stable, low and very bare,
    A little child in a manger.
The oxen knew Him, had Him in their care,
    To men He was a stranger.
The safety of the world was lying there,
    And the world's danger.

Mary Elizabeth Coleridge

The Oxen

Christmas Eve, and twelve of the clock.
'Now they are all on their knees,'
An elder said, as we sat in a flock,
By the embers in fireside ease.

We pictured the meek mild creatures, where
They dwelt in their strawy pen,
Nor did it occur to one of us there
To doubt they were kneeling then.

So fair a fancy few would weave
In these years! Yet, I feel
If someone said, on Christmas Eve,
'Come; see the oxen kneel

'In the lonely barton by yonder coomb,
Our childhood used to know,'
I should go with him in the gloom,
Hoping it might be so.

Thomas Hardy

The Barn

'I am tired of this barn!' said the colt.
'And every day it snows.
Outside there's no grass any more
And icicles grow on my nose.
I am tired of hearing the cows
Breathing and talking together.
I am sick of these clucking hens.
I *hate* stables and winter weather!'

'Hush, little colt,' said the mare.
'And a story I will tell
Of a barn like this one of ours
And the wonders that there befell.
It was weather much like this,
And the beasts stood as we stand now
In the warm good dark of the barn –
A horse and an ass and a cow.'

'And sheep?' asked the colt. 'Yes, sheep,
And a pig and a goat and a hen.
All of the beasts of the barnyard,
The usual servants of men.
And into their midst came a lady
And she was cold as death,
But the animals leaned above her
And made her warm with their breath.

'There was her baby born
And laid to sleep in the hay,
While music flooded the rafters
And the barn was as light as day.
And angels and kings and shepherds
Came to worship the babe from afar,
But we looked at him first of all creatures
By the bright strange light of a star!'

Elizabeth Coatsworth

Mice in the Hay

out of the lamplight
  whispering worshipping
the mice in the hay

timid eyes pearl-bright
  whispering worshipping
whisking quick and away

they were there that night
  whispering worshipping
smaller than snowflakes are

quietly made their way
  whispering worshipping
close to the manger

yes, they were afraid
  whispering worshipping
as the journey was made

from a dark corner
  whispering worshipping
scuttling together

But He smiled to see them
  whispering worshipping
there in the lamplight

stretched out His hand to them
  they saw the baby King
hurried back out of sight
  whispering worshipping

Leslie Norris

Angels' Song

FIRST ANGEL   Fear not, shepherds, for I bring
Tidings of a new-born King –
Not in castle, not in keep,
Nor in tower tall and steep;
Not in manor-house or hall,
But a humble ox's stall.

SECOND ANGEL   Underneath a standing star
And where sheep and cattle are,
In a bed of straw and hay
God's own Son is born this day.
If to Bethlehem you go,
This the truth you soon shall know.

THIRD ANGEL   And as signal and as sign,
Sure as all the stars that shine,
You shall find him, shepherds all,
Swaddled in a baby-shawl;
And the joyful news will share
With good people everywhere.

SECOND ANGEL   Therefore, listen as we cry:

THREE ANGELS   Glory be to God on high,
And his gifts of love and peace
To his people never cease.

Charles Causley

Carol of Patience

Shepherds armed with staff and sling,
Ranged along a steep hillside,
Watch for their anointed King
By all prophets prophesied –
 Sing patience, patience,
 Only still have patience.

Hour by hour they scrutinize
Comet, planet, planet, star,
Till the oldest shepherd sighs,
'I am frail and he is far.'
 Sing patience, patience,
 Only still have patience.

'Born, they say, a happy child;
Grown, a man of grief to be,
From all careless joys exiled,
Rooted in eternity.'
 Sing patience, patience,
 Only still have patience.

Then another shepherd said:
'Yonder lights are Bethlehem;
There young David raised his head
Destined for the diadem.'
 Sing patience, patience,
 Only still have patience.

Cried the youngest shepherd: 'There
Our Redeemer comes tonight,
Comes with starlight on his hair,
With his brow exceeding bright.'
 Sing patience, patience,
 Only still have patience.

'Sacrifice no lamb nor kid,
Let such foolish fashions pass;
In a manger find him hid,
Breathed upon by ox and ass.'
    Sing patience, patience,
    Only still have patience.

Dance for him and laugh and sing,
Watch him mercifully smile,
Dance although tomorrow bring
Every plague that plagued the Nile.
    Sing patience, patience,
    Only still have patience.

Robert Graves

Moonless darkness stands between

Moonless darkness stands between.
Past, O Past, no more be seen!
But the Bethlehem star may lead me
To the sight of Him who freed me
From the self that I have been.
Make me pure, Lord: Thou art holy;
Make me meek, Lord: Thou wert lowly;
Now beginning, and alway:
Now begin, on Christmas day.

Gerard Manley Hopkins

The Shepherd's Tale

Woman, you'll never credit what
My two eyes saw this night . . .
But first of all we'll have a drop,
It's freezing now, all right.

It was the queerest going-on
That I did e'er behold:
A holy child out in the barn,
A baby all in gold.

Now let's get started on the soup,
And let me tell it you,
For though there's not a thing made up,
It still seems hardly true.

There he was laid upon the straw,
Will you dish up the stew?
The ass did bray, the hens did craw,
I'll have some cabbage too.

First there was a king from Prussia,
At least that's how he looked,
Then there was the king of Russia.
This stew's been overcooked.

There they were kneeling on the ground.
Come, have a bite to eat.
First I just stared and stood around.
Have just a taste of meat!

Well, one of them he ups and says
A long speech – kind of funny.
Here, what about that last new cheese,
Is it still runny?

The little 'un, wise as wise could be,
Just didn't care for that.
But he was pleased as punch with me
When I took off me hat.

I took his little fists in mine,
In front of all those nobs.
Fetch us a jug of our best wine
My dear, we'll wet our gobs.

That very instant, as if I'd
Had a good swig of drink,
I felt a great warm joy inside,
But why, I cannot think.

Ah, this wine's the stuff, by Mary!
When he's grown up a bit,
That little fellow, just you see,
He shall have some of it!

We might have all been knelt there yet,
Put a Yule log on the fire,
But suddenly he starts to fret –
He'd begun to tire.

Then 'Sirs,' his mother she did say,
'It grieves me to remind
You that it's time to go away
When you have been so kind.

'But see, how sleepy he's become,
He's crying, let him rest.
You all know how to find our home
Each one's a welcome guest.'

And so in silence we went out,
But the funniest thing –
Those three fine kings,
Did wish me good-morning!

You see, love, that's how it began.
The God born on the earth
This night's no ordinary one.
Let's celebrate his birth!

James Kirkup
From the French of Raoul Ponchon

The Shepherd's Dog

Out on the windy hill
Under that sudden star
A blaze of radiant light
Frightened my master.

He got up, left our sheep,
Tramped over the moor.
And I, following,
Came to this open door,

Sidled in, settled down,
Head on my paws,
Glad to be here, away
From the wind's sharpness.

Such warmth is in this shed,
Such comfort from this Child,
That I forget my hard life,
Ignore the harsh world,

And see on my master's face
The same joy I possess,
The knowledge of peace,
True happiness.

Leslie Norris

Shepherds' Carol

Three practical farmers from back of the dale –
    Under the high sky –
On a Saturday night said 'So long' to their sheep
That were bottom of dyke and fast asleep –
    When the stars came out in the Christmas sky.

They called at the pub for a gill of ale –
    Under the high sky –
And they found in the stable, stacked with the corn,
The latest arrival, newly-born –
    When the stars came out in the Christmas sky.

They forgot their drink, they rubbed their eyes –
    Under the high sky –
They were tough as leather and ripe as a cheese
But they dropped like a ten year-old down on their knees –
    When the stars came out in the Christmas sky.

They ran out in the yard to swap their news –
    Under the high sky –
They pulled off their caps and roused a cheer
To greet a spring lamb before New Year –
    When the stars came out in the Christmas sky.

Norman Nicholson

Christmas Day

Last night in the open shippen
   The Infant Jesus lay,
While cows stood at the hay-crib
   Twitching the sweet hay.

As I trudged through the snow-fields
   That lay in their own light,
A thorn-bush with its shadow
   Stood doubled on the night.

And I stayed on my journey
   To listen to the cheep
Of a small bird in the thorn-bush
   I woke from its puffed sleep.

The bright stars were my angels
   And with the heavenly host
I sang praise to the Father,
   The Son and Holy Ghost.

Andrew Young

Sailor's Carol

Lord, the snowful sky
   In this pale December
Fingers my clear eye
   Lest seeing, I remember

Not the naked baby
   Weeping in the stable
Nor the singing boys
   All round my table,

Not the dizzy star
   Bursting on the pane
Nor the leopard sun
   Pawing the rain.

Only the deep garden
   Where green lilies grow,
The sailors rolling
   In the sea's blue snow.

Charles Causley

The Carol of the Poor Children

We are the poor children, come out to see the sights
On this day of all days, on this night of nights,
The stars in merry parties are dancing in the sky,
A fine star, a new star, is shining on high!

We are the poor children, our lips are frosty blue,
We cannot sing our carol as well as rich folk do,
Our bellies are so empty we have no singing voice,
But this night of all nights good children must rejoice.

We do rejoice, we do rejoice, as hard as we can try,
A fine star, a new star is shining in the sky!
And while we sing our carol, we think of the delight
The happy kings and shepherds make in Bethlehem tonight.

Are we naked, mother, and are we starving-poor –
Oh, see what gifts the kings have brought outside the stable door,
Are we cold, mother, the ass will give his hay
To make the manger warm and keep the cruel winds away.

We are the poor children, but not so poor who sing
Our carol with our voiceless hearts to greet the new-born king,
On this night of all nights, when in the frosty sky
A new star, a kind star is shining on high!

Richard Middleton

St Stephen's Day

Yesterday the gentle
Story: the summoning star,
Shepherd and beast and king
In the enchanted ring,
The moment still with awe.

Shepherd and beast and king
Wince at a cry:
It is no newborn cry
For he is asleep,
But a cry alerting night.

Who saw the hanging star
Shudder and fall?
I, Stephen, saw
Fragments of hot stone
Whistle down, smite the earth.

Stones thud on flesh,
The bestial mob howls,
No kings are here to witness.
Yesterday birth blood,
Today pulped flesh and death blood

Streaming from broken eyes:
Yet the triumphant cry
I see my God.
So was the first day
After the gentle birth.

Patric Dickinson

The Feast o' Saint Stephen

Hearken all ye, 'tis the feast o' Saint Stephen,
Mind that ye keep it this holy even.
Open your door an' greet ye the stranger
For ye mind that the wee Lord had naught but a manger.

Feed ye the hungry an' rest ye the weary,
This ye must do for the sake of Our Mary.
'Tis well that ye mind – ye who sit by the fire –
That the Lord He was born in a dark and cold byre.

Ruth Sawyer

The Feast of Stephen

After the midnight unfolding of the White Rose
Under the windblown stars; after the heartsease,
A bloodstain on the altar-cloth, veiling the cup
Red for Stephen's martyrdom.

After the silver fanfares of the Angelic heralds
Crying a truce and comfort, after this
The edged stones, the blade more bitter than flame;
These too, gifts of the Incarnate.

After the birth, the sowing, the bleak memorial
Of death the Harvester; after the swaddling clothes
The sweat-stained garments, heavy with dust and destiny
Stacked at the feet of Saul.

Kevin Nichols

Kings came Riding

Kings came riding
  One, two, and three,
Over the desert
  And over the sea.

One in a ship
  With a silver mast;
The fishermen wondered
  As he went past.

One on a horse
  With a saddle of gold;
The children came running
  To behold.

One came walking,
  Over the sand,
With a casket of treasure
  Held in his hand.

All the people
  Said, 'Where go they?'
But the kings went forward
  All through the day.

Night came on
  As those kings went by;
They shone like the gleaming
  Stars in the sky.

Charles Williams

The Wise Men ask the Children the Way

'Dear children,' they asked in every town
Three kings from the land of the sun,
'Which is the road to Bethlehem?'
But neither the old nor the young

Could tell, and the kings rode on;
Their guide was a star in the air
Of gold, which glittered ahead of them,
So clear, so clear.

The star stood still over Joseph's house.
They all of them stepped in;
The good ox lowed and the little child cried,
And the kings began to sing.

Heinrich Heine
Translated by Geoffrey Grigson

Camels of the Kings

'The Camels, the Kings' Camels, Haie-aie!
Saddles of polished leather, stained red and purple,
Pommels inlaid with ivory and beaten gold,
Bridles of silk embroidery, worked with flowers.
The Camels, the Kings' Camels!'

We are groomed with silver combs,
We are washed with perfumes.
The grain of richest Africa is fed to us,
Our dishes are silver.
Like cloth-of-gold glisten our sleek pelts.
Of all camels, we alone carry the Kings!
Do you wonder that we are proud?
That our hooded eyes are contemptuous?

As we sail past the tented villages
They beat their copper gongs after us.
'The windswift, the desert racers. See them!
Faster than gazelles, faster than hounds,
Haie-aie! The Camels, the Kings' Camels!'
The sand drifts in puffs behind us,
The glinting quartz, the fine, hard grit.
Do you wonder that we look down our noses?
Do you wonder we flare our superior nostrils?

All night we have run under the moon,
Without effort, breathing lightly,
Smooth as a breeze over the desert floor,
One white star our compass.
We have come to no palace, no place
Of towers and minarets and the calling of servants,
But a poor stable in a poor town.
So why are we bending our crested necks?
Why are our proud heads bowed
And our eyes closed meekly?
Why are we outside this hovel,
Humbly and awkwardly kneeling?
How is it that we know the world is changed?

Leslie Norris

Journey of the Magi

'A cold coming we had of it,
Just the worst time of the year
For a journey, and such a long journey:
The ways deep and the weather sharp,
The very dead of winter.'
And the camels galled, sore-footed, refractory,
Lying down in the melting snow.
There were times we regretted
The summer palaces on slopes, the terraces,
And the silken girls bringing sherbet.

Then the camel men cursing and grumbling
And running away, and wanting their liquor and women,
And the night-fires going out, and the lack of shelters,
And the cities hostile and the towns unfriendly
And the villages dirty and charging high prices:
A hard time we had of it.
At the end we preferred to travel all night,
Sleeping in snatches,
With the voices singing in our ears, saying
That this was all folly.
Then at dawn we came down to a temperate valley,
Wet, below the snow line, smelling of vegetation;
With a running stream and a water-mill beating the darkness,
And three trees on the low sky,
And an old white horse galloped away in the meadow.
Then we came to a tavern with vine-leaves over the lintel,
Six hands at an open door dicing for pieces of silver,
And feet kicking the empty wine-skins.
But there was no information, and so we continued
And arrived at evening, not a moment too soon
Finding the place; it was (you may say) satisfactory.
All this was a long time ago, I remember,
And I would do it again, but set down
This set down
This: were we led all that way for
Birth or Death? There was a Birth, certainly,
We had evidence and no doubt. I had seen birth and death,
But had thought they were different; this Birth was
Hard and bitter agony for us, like Death, our death.
We returned to our places, these kingdoms,
But no longer at ease here, in the old dispensation,
With an alien people clutching their gods.
I should be glad of another death.

T. S. Eliot

The Adoration of the Magi

It was the arrival of the kings
that caught us unawares;
we'd looked in on the woman in the barn,
curiosity you could call it,
something to do on a cold winter's night;
we'd wished her well –
that was the best we could do, she was in pain,
and the next thing we knew
she was lying on the straw
– the little there was of it –
and there was this baby in her arms.

It was, as I say, the kings
that caught us unawares . . .
Women have babies every other day,
not that we are there –
let's call it a common occurrence though,
giving birth. But kings
appearing in a stable with a
'Is this the place?' and kneeling,
each with his gift held out towards the child!

They didn't even notice us.
Their robes trailed on the floor,
rich, lined robes that money couldn't buy.
What must this child be
to bring kings from distant lands
with costly incense and gold?
What could a tiny baby make of that?

And what were we to make of
was it angels falling through the air,
entwined and falling as if from the rafters
to where the gaze of the kings met the child's
— assuming the child could see?

What would the mother do with the gift?
What would become of the child?
And we'll never admit there are angels

or that somewhere between
one man's eyes and another's
is a holy place, a space where a king could be
at one with a naked child,
at one with an astonished soldier.

Christopher Pilling

The Mystic Magi

(It is chronicled in an old Armenian myth, that the Wise Men of the
East were none other than the three sons of Noah, and that they were
raised from the dead to represent, and to do homage for, all mankind in
the cave of Bethlehem.)

Three ancient men in Bethlehem's cave
　With awful wonder stand:
A voice had called them from their grave,
　In some far Eastern land.

They lived: they trod the former earth,
　When the old waters swelled,
The Ark, that womb of second birth,
　Their house and lineage held.

Pale Japhet bows the knee with gold,
  Bright Sem sweet incense brings,
And Cham the myrrh his fingers hold:
  Lo! the three orient Kings.

Types of the total earth, they hailed
  The signal's starry frame:
Shuddering with second life, they quailed
  At the Child Jesu's Name.

Then slow the Patriarchs turned and trod,
  And this their parting sigh:
'Our eyes have seen the living God,
  And now – once more to die.'

Robert Stephen Hawker

The Huron Carol

'Twas in the moon of winter-time,
   When all the birds had fled,
That mighty Gitchi Manitou
   Sent angel choirs instead;
Before their light the stars grew dim,
And wandering hunters heard the hymn:
   Jesus your King is born.

Within a lodge of broken bark
   The tender Babe was found,
A ragged robe of rabbit skin
   Enwrapped his beauty round:
But as the hunter braves drew nigh,
The angel-song rang loud and high.
   Jesus your King is born.

The earliest moon of winter-time
   Is not so round and fair
As was the ring of glory on
   The helpless Infant there.
The chiefs from far before him knelt
With gifts of fox and beaver-pelt.
   Jesus your King is born.

O children of the forest free,
   O sons of Manitou,
The Holy Child of earth and heaven
   Is born today for you.
Come kneel before the radiant Boy,
Who brings you beauty, peace and joy.
   Jesus your King is born.

J. Edgar Middleton
(Canadian carol, originally French)

Gitchi Manitou: the supreme God.

What the Donkey Saw

No room in the inn, of course,
And not that much in the stable,
What with the shepherds, Magi, Mary,
Joseph, the heavenly host –
Not to mention the baby
Using our manger as a cot.
You couldn't have squeezed another cherub in
For love or money.

Still, in spite of the overcrowding,
I did my best to make them feel wanted.
I could see the baby and I
Would be going places together.

U. A. Fanthorpe

A Ballad of Christmas

It was about the deep of night,
  And still was earth and sky,
When in the moonlight, dazzling bright,
  Three ghosts came riding by.

Beyond the sea – beyond the sea,
  Lie kingdoms for them all:
I wot their steeds trod wearily –
  The journey is not small.

By rock and desert, sand and stream,
  They footsore late did go:
Now, like a sweet and blessed dream,
  Their path was deep with snow.

Shining like hoar-frost, rode they on,
  Three ghosts in earth's array:
It was about the hour when wan
  Night turns at hint of day.

For bloody was each hand, and dark
  With death each orbless eye; –
It was three Traitors mute and stark
  Came riding silent by.

Silver their raiment and their spurs,
  And silver-shod their feet,
And silver-pale each face that stared
  Into the moonlight sweet.

And he upon the left that rode
  Was Pilate, Prince of Rome,
Whose journey once lay far abroad,
  And now was nearing home.

And he upon the right that rode,
  Herod of Salem sate,
Whose mantle dipped in children's blood
  Shone clear as Heaven's gate.

And he, these twain betwixt, that rode
   Was clad as white as wool,
Dyed in the Mercy of his God,
   White was he crown to sole.

Throned 'mid a myriad Saints in bliss
   Rise shall the Babe of Heaven
To shine on these three ghosts, iwis,
   Smit through with sorrows seven;

Babe of the Blessed Trinity
   Shall smile their steeds to see:
Herod and Pilate riding by,
   And Judas, one of three.

Walter de la Mare

The Holy Innocents

Listen, the hay-bells tinkle as the cart
Wavers on rubber tyres along the tar
And cindered ice below the burlap mill
And ale-wife run. The oxen drool and start
In wonder at the fenders of a car,
And blunder hugely up St Peter's hill.
These are the undefiled by woman – their
Sorrow is not the sorrow of this world:
King Herod shrieking vengeance at the curled
Up knees of Jesus choking in the air,

A king of speechless clods and infants. Still
The world out-Herods Herod; and the year,
The nineteen-hundred forty-fifth of grace,
Lumbers with losses up the clinkered hill
Of our purgation; and the oxen near
The worn foundations of their resting-place,
The holy manger where their bed is corn
And holly torn for Christmas. If they die,
As Jesus, in the harness, who will mourn?
Lamb of the shepherds, Child, how still you lie.

Robert Lowell

Innocent's Song

Who's that knocking on the window,
Who's that standing at the door,
What are all those presents
Lying on the kitchen floor?

Who is the smiling stranger
With hair as white as gin,
What is he doing with the children
And who could have let him in?

Why has he rubies on his fingers,
A cold, cold crown on his head,
Why, when he caws his carol,
Does the salty snow run red?

Why does he ferry my fireside
As a spider on a thread,
His fingers made of fuses
And his tongue of gingerbread?

Why does the world before him
Melt in a million suns,
Why do his yellow, yearning eyes
Burn like saffron buns?

Watch where he comes walking
Out of the Christmas flame,
Dancing, double talking:

Herod is his name.

Charles Causley

Clap Your Hands for Herod

We
little children in our shifts
long since washed clean
of bloodstains
have gathered together
as we were instructed
and are making ready to greet King Herod

For us the massacred innocents
a special place was kept in heaven
Here there are woods
full of undergrowth and game
and grey caves we may creep into

We the smallest of the dead
once believed in our ignorance
that King Herod
was a wicked man
who had us killed
from mere brutality and lack of heart
But we were told:
Look at the woods you are living in
even the smallest song-birds
snap up insects coloured like the rainbow
to be fattened
for the wild cat's jaws
little snakes swallow mice
big ones rabbits and hares
and when the wolf that devours the sheep
falls sick he is torn to pieces by his brothers
And so it is with the plants and flowers
one strangles another's growth
seizes its piece of earth
and share of the sun

Worse by far
is it among human beings
who besides animal malice
have hatred one for another
and the cunning
to perfect their power to kill

These things they said to us
and we pale-faced little angels
gulping in terror
cowered closer to the tree-roots
and gave thanks
that here in these woods thirsting for blood
we were not really alive
and they went on:
There is no love among men
nor in the world of the living
But King Herod
loved above all else
you little mortals white as the lamb
and therefore freed you from life
that you might be spared
its limitless horrors
Be grateful to your deliverer
and if he comes among you
greet him with clapping and song

And there were among us some
who at that moment cried out
that in life there is love
their palms kept the memory of it
and that King Herod
was a foul murderer
who ought to be quartered
with a butcher's axe
and his parts
thrown to the wild beasts
but others of us
stopped their mouths
for we were full of joy
and gratitude towards the king

and we wept
tears of remorse for the lies and slander
in which we had come to believe
and we lifted up translucent hands
in thanksgiving for the truth shown to us
and we are gathered here for the last time
around the sacrificial altar
preparing to sing praise
and waiting to clap our hands
for Herod

who is coming to kill us once again

Twelfth Night

Josef Hanzlik
Translated by Ian Milner

Our candles, lit, re-lit, have gone down now:
There were the dry twigs tipped with buds of fire,
But red and white have twisted into air,
The little shadow stills its to and fro.

We draw familiar faces from the wall
But all is part of a dismantling dark
Which works upon the heart that must not break,
Upon the carried thing that must not fall.

Needles are shivered from the golden bough.
Our leaves and paper nothings are decayed
And all amazements of the Phoenix breed
Are cupboarded in dust, dull row on row,

While branchwork set upon a whitened ground
Climbs out into a vortex of wild flame.
The substance of this deep Midwinter dream:
A scale of ash upon a frozen wind.

Our candles, lit, re-lit, have gone down now:
Only the tears, the veils, the hanging tree
Whose burning gauze thins out across the sky,
Whose brightness dies to image. And the snow.

Peter Scupham

On the Thirteenth Day of Christmas

On the thirteenth day of Christmas
    I saw King Jesus go
About the plain beyond my pane
    Wearing his cap of snow.

Sad was his brow as the snow-sky
    While all the world made merry,
In the black air his wounds burned bare
    As the fire in the holly berry.

At all the weeping windows
    The greedy children gather
And laugh at the clown in his white nightgown
    In the wicked winter weather.

I dragged the desperate city,
    I swagged the combing light,
I stood alone at the empty throne
    At the ninth hour of night.

On the thirteenth day of Christmas
    When the greasy guns bellow
His eye is dry as the splitting sky
    And his face is yellow.

Charles Causley

Carol for the Last Christmas Eve

The first night, the first night,
   The night that Christ was born,
His mother looked in his eyes and saw
   Her maker in her son.

The twelfth night, the twelfth night,
   After Christ was born,
The Wise Men found the child and knew
   Their search had just begun.

Eleven thousand, two fifty nights,
   After Christ was born,
A dead man hung in the child's light
   And the sun went down at noon.

Six hundred thousand or thereabout nights,
   After Christ was born,
I look at you and you look at me
But the sky is too dark for us to see
   And the world waits for the sun.

But the last night, the last night,
   Since ever Christ was born,
What his mother knew will be known again,
And what was found by the Three Wise Men,
And the sun will rise and so may we,
   On the last morn, on Christmas Morn,
Umpteen hundred and eternity.

Norman Nicholson

Glad Christmas comes, and every hearth
Makes room to bid him welcome now . . .

Wassailing Song

Wisselton, wasselton, who lives here?
We've come to taste your Christmas beer.
Up the kitchen and down the hall,
Holly, ivy, and mistletoe;
A peck of apples will serve us all,
Give us some apples and let us go.

Up with your stocking, on with your shoe,
If you haven't any apples, money will do.
My carol's done, and I must be gone,
No longer can I stay here.
God bless you all, great and small,
And send you a happy new year.

Traditional

Yule Log

Come, bring with a noise,
My merrie, merrie boyes,
The Christmas Log to the firing;
While my good Dame, she
Bids ye all be free;
And drink to your hearts' desiring.

With the last yeeres brand
Light the new block, and
For good successe in his spending,
On your Psaltries play,
That sweet luck may
Come while the log is a-teending.

Drink now the strong Beere,
Cut the white loafe here,
The while the meat is a-shredding;
For the rare Mince-Pie
And the Plums stand by
To fill the paste that's a-kneading.

Robert Herrick

Heap On More Wood!

Heap on more wood! – the wind is chill;
But let it whistle as it will,
We'll keep our Christmas merry still.
Each age has deem'd the new-born year
The fittest time for festal cheer:
Even, heathen yet, the savage Dane
At Iol more deep the mead did drain;
High on the beach his galleys drew,
And feasted all his pirate crew;
Then in his low and pine-built hall,
Where shields and axes deck'd the wall,
They gorged upon the half dress'd steer;
Caroused in seas of sable beer;
While round, in brutal jest, were thrown
The half-gnaw'd rib, and marrow-bone:
Or listen'd all, in grim delight,
While Scalds yell'd out the joys of fight.
Then forth, in frenzy, would they hie,
While wildly loose their red locks fly,
And dancing round the blazing pile,
They make such barbarous mirth the while,
As best might to the mind recall
The boisterous joys of Odin's hall.

Walter Scott

Christmas Shopping

Spending beyond their income on gifts for Christmas –
Swing doors and crowded lifts and draperied jungles –
What shall we buy for our husbands and sons
    Different from last year?

Foxes hang by their noses behind plate glass –
Scream of macaws across festoons of paper –
Only the faces on the boxes of chocolates are free
    From boredom and crowsfeet.

Sometimes a chocolate box girl escapes in the flesh,
Lightly manoeuvres the crowd, trilling with laughter;
After a couple of years her feet and brain will
    Tire like the others.

The great windows marshal their troops for assault on the purse,
Something-and-eleven the yard, hoodwinking logic,
The eleventh hour draining the gurgling pennies
    Down the conduits

Down to the sewers of money — rats and marshgas
Bubbling in maundering music under the pavement;
Here go the hours of routine, the weight on our eyelids —
   Pennies on corpses.

While over the street in the centrally heated public
Library dwindling figures with sloping shoulders
And hands in pockets, weighted in the boots like chessmen,
   Stare at the printed

Columns of ads, the quickset road to riches,
Starting at a little and temporary but once we're
Started who knows whether we shan't continue,
   Salaries rising,

Rising like a salmon against the bullnecked river,
Bound for the spawning ground of care-free days —
Good for a fling before the golden wheels run
   Down to a standstill.

And Christ is born — the nursery glad with baubles,
Alive with light and washable paint and children's
Eyes expects as its due the accidental
   Loot of a system.

Smell of the South – oranges in silver paper,
Dates and ginger, the benison of firelight,
The blue flames dancing round the brandied raisins,
    Smiles from above them,

Hands from above them as of gods but really
These their parents, always seen from below, them-
Selves are always anxious looking across the
    Fence to the future –

Out there lies the future gathering quickly
Its black momentum; through the tubes of London
The dead wind blows the crowds like beasts in flight from
    Fire in the forest.

The little fir trees palpitate with candles
In hundreds of chattering households where the suburb
Straggles like nervous handwriting, the margin
    Blotted with smokestacks.

Further out on the coast the lighthouse moves its
Arms of light through the fog that wads our welfare,
Moves its arms like a giant Swedish drill whose
    Mind is a vacuum.

Louis MacNeice

The Crib

They are making a crèche at the Saturday morning classes
For the Christmas party: scissors and paper vie
With fingers and plasticine until there are masses
Of sheep and shepherds that kneel and stand and lie,

And cotton-batting angels with cellophane wings
And a golded cardboard star and string to guide it
And pipe-cleaner camels carrying tinfoil kings
And a real straw manger with Joseph and Mary beside it.

But the manger is empty. The Saturday classes contain
So many different faiths, there is a danger
Of giving offence; there was once no room in the inn,
Now there is no room for him in the manger.

Of course he will understand, his love is hearty
Enough to forgive and forget the being slighted
And true enough not to offend at the birthday party
By showing up where he is uninvited.

Besides he is long accustomed to the manners
Of centuries that consecrate the snub
Of Christmas honoured, not the one it honours.
Strange they should trouble to give the crèche a crib.

Robert Finch

Journey Back to Christmas

I ran to the church,
Ran all the way
With hay
From the pet shop
For our Christmas play.
I'd had to wait for the hay
And rehearsal was over. I was late.
Panting up the steps I heard the high church clock strike four –
They'd all gone!
I pushed the thick door
And was suddenly in
Quiet.
All the town's din
Gone.
One yellow light
Shone
Beyond the long, high, shadowy place
On a tablecloth with lace.
'That's the altar,' our teacher'd said.
Now she saw me, smiled and called,
'Got the hay, Tim? Good. Now come and spread
It carefully about.'

She went out
And I was alone
In that big tent of stone.
It smelt of dust and flowers.
I walked along a lane between seats to the manger –
That wasn't the church's. That was ours.
We'd bought hardboard, made a trough,
Four legs of batten, sand-papered off –
The trough felt cold so I filled it with hay,
Warm hay, smelling of rabbits and summer,
I put more
On the floor
And wondered if that first Christmas Day
Was anything like our play –
Where Jesus is only a doll.

Was there a light
On Christmas Eve night
To show Mary and Joseph the way
When they were seeking a place to stay
In Bethlehem nearly two thousand years ago?
Was there snow?
Every little inn in Bethlehem that night
Was packed tight with strangers
And no-one in any street
Could find a room or even a bed
To greet
Mary, whose baby – Jesus – would be born soon.
Was she afraid? Was there a frosty moon?
Then someone at last was able
To offer his stable.
Was he kind? Did he call his wife to help?
Had he a dog to snap and yelp,
Scenting danger
Because Joseph was a stranger?
Did the manger
In that stable smell as sweet as ours?
Did Mary's donkey push a grey-brown face
Into that manger?

I put mine in ours
And sniffed up ghosts of flowers –
I coughed and the sound
Went round and round in the shadows.
The church felt higher, full of darkness, cold and wide,
Miles from the street outside.

Under the light by the altar was a black chair.
I put it by the manger for Jean –
She's Mary in our play – she's fair.
And Joseph is Mark.
He's dark.
Were they really dark? or fair?
And was there a stool or chair
For Mary in that stable reeking of camels?
Was she frightened when the flickering lantern's light
Showed her – very close – a donkey's shining eyes, a cow's curled horn?
Did someone hold her hand until Jesus was born?

I put hay on the black seat
And more where Mary'd put her feet,
Some on the floor where she might lie.
Did the real Mary cry?
I stood back then to see
The whole scene where our play would be.
I act the part of a shepherd,
A young one,
Old Ezra's son.
And when the angels sing about god's son
Being born to Mary
I hear them first

And I call
To the others,
'Listen, all!
Hear the night sky burst
With joy
Because this boy,
God's son,
Is born today!'
I like saying that.
I like our play.
But I don't like the doll meant to be Jesus,
Pink and wrapped in a white sheet,
Tight and neat,
Still and flat.
Jesus wasn't like that!
Was he?
He was lively,
Soft, red and wrinkled, very small,
With tiny toenails.
Did he kick and bawl
Till Mary wrapped him in her shawl?
Did she hear the shepherds whispering outside,
Cold feet, wrapped in hide,
Crouching on frozen mud?
I looked into the long dark of the church
And saw those shepherds – Well, I thought I did –
Saw them lurch
Against each other with tiredness,
There were six. There are six in our play.
A tall one, black-bearded, and his brother,
An old man and his son,
A round-faced one
And one other,

A boy like somebody I'd met.

The frost had melted on his coat;
His hair was wet.
He shook his head, looked up – and suddenly
I stood stone-still!
That boy I'd seen
Was me

– Or might have been –
I saw him smile and run and kneel at Mary's feet
On the hay I'd put by the seat.

'Please lady, show us the King!
The angels sent us here – angels, lady.
We've come, hurrying.
Old Sam here's bust himself trying
To be first to greet your son.
Please lady, I ain't lying.
I don't know much but I heard that singing!
We all heard it, didn't we? dong-dinging
It was – all clap-banging round the stars
Like bells and pipes and drums and bird calls
And all music. It made old Sam here dance.
It did, didn't it, Sam?
Show us the King, ma'am.
We never had much to bring
But we brought what we could
And that's all good.
Lady, show us the King.
God's son, the angels said
Though I don't see
How that can be,
You being ordinary
Though your face is sweet
Show us the King, lady.'

I saw and heard from where I stood,
Saw old Sam put out a hand, knobbly like wood,
And touch the boy's arm.

'Quiet, Tim. Be good.
He ain't a cheeky boy, ma'am.
He've brought ya a lamb,
His own,
Little black 'un –
Be a fine sheep when that's grown.
And here's cheese, coupla fleeces and a goat skin.
– Hope that's all right – us comin' in.
You see the message was that you'd be here
Waiting with your baby to bring cheer
To us shepherds – and all men.
So we come immediately – Simeon, John, Ezra, Saul and young Tim –
Couldn't leave him.
Said he had to see the King
So we let him come.
What's the baby's name, now, Tim?'
'Jesus. Mary is that right?'
Mary nodded.

Then I saw old Sam
Pick up the baby on his arm
As he might a new lamb.

'I'll do him no harm, lady.
Little marvel, ain't ya!
You're the one the angels sang about.
Come and see the baby, Tim.'

Then Tim – who looked like me –
Touched the baby.
I couldn't see
Jesus' face,
I wished I was in the boy's place.
I wished the baby in our play was real,
A real baby Jesus, alive and warm to feel.
Perhaps I'd understand
What son of God means
If I touched him with my hand.

The shadows swallowed the shepherds
My feet felt cold
Hay's not very warm on a stone floor.
I walked along that lane towards the door.
The clock wheezed overhead,
Ready to chime.

'Still here, Tim?
Do you know the time?
You must be cold.'

'You'd think they could have found
Something better than hay
For a new-born King
On a winter's day!'
From the door where we stood
We looked at the manger under the light –
'Yes, Tim, you would.'

Gwen Dunn

Carol

Deep in the fading leaves of night
There lay the flower that darkness knows,
Till winter stripped and brought to light
The most incomparable Rose
That blows, that blows.

The flashing mirrors of the snow
Keep turning and returning still:
To see the lovely child below
And hold him is their only will;
Keep still, keep still.

And to let go his very cry
The clinging echoes are so slow
That still his wail they multiply
Though he lie singing now below,
So low, so low.

Even the doves forget to grieve
And gravely to his greetings fly
And the lone places that they leave
All follow and are standing by
On high, on high.

W. R. Rodgers

How to Paint a Perfect Christmas

Above, you paint the sky
delicate as maidenhair.
Below, pour a little darkness
heated to room temperature
or slightly more.

With a cat's claw in the dark
scratch out a little tree,
the finest tree in the world,
finer than any forester
could ever imagine.

And the tree itself
will light up
and the whole picture purr
with green joy,
with purple hope.

Right. But now you must
put under the tree
the
real big thing,
the thing you most want in the world;
the thing pop-singers
call happiness.

It's easy enough for a cat,
a cat will put a mouse there,
Colonel Blimp will line up
the largest jet-propelled halberd
which shoots and bangs and salutes,
a sparrow will gather
a few stalks for its nest,
mister junior clerk will submit
a stuffed file tied with red tape,
a butterfly will put there
a new rubber peacock's eye,
but what will *you* put there?

You think and think
till the day grows grey,
till the river almost runs out,
till even the bulbs begin to yawn,
you think

and finally

there in the darkness you blot out
a hazy white spot,
a bit like a florin,
a bit like a ship,
a bit like the Moon,
a bit like the beautiful face
of someone (who?) else,

a hazy white spot,
perhaps more like emptiness,
like the negation of something,
like non-pain,
like non-fear,
like non-worry,

a hazy white spot,
and you go to bed
and say to yourself,
yes, now I know how to do it,
yes, now I know,
yes,
next time
I shall paint
the most perfect Christmas
that ever was.

Miroslav Holub

Translated by George Theiner and Ian Milner

Noel: Christmas Eve, 1913

A frosty Christmas Eve
  when the stars were shining
Fared I forth alone
  where westward falls the hill,
And from many a village
  in the water'd valley
Distant music reach'd me
  peals of bells aringing:
The constellated sounds
  ran sprinkling on earth's floor
As the dark vault above
  with stars was spangled o'er.
Then sped my thought to keep
  that first Christmas of all
When the shepherds watching
  by their folds ere the dawn
Heard music in the fields
  and marveling could not tell
Whether it were angels
  or the bright stars singing.
Now blessed be the tow'rs
  that crown England so fair
That stand up strong in prayer
  unto God for our souls:
Blessed be their founders
  (said I) an' our country folk
Who are ringing for Christ
  in the belfries to-night
With arms lifted to clutch
  the rattling ropes that race
Into the dark above
  and the mad romping din.
But to me heard afar
  it was starry music
Angels' song, comforting
  as the comfort of Christ
When he spake tenderly
  to his sorrowful flock:

The old words came to me
by the riches of time
Mellow'd and transfigured
as I stood on the hill
Heark'ning in the aspect
of th' eternal silence.

Robert Bridges

Eddi's Service

Eddi, priest of St Wilfrid
   In the chapel at Manhood End,
Ordered a midnight service
   For such as cared to attend.

But the Saxons were keeping Christmas,
   And the night was stormy as well.
Nobody came to service,
   Though Eddi rang the bell.

'Wicked weather for walking,'
   Said Eddi of Manhood End.
'But I must go on with the service
   For such as care to attend.'

The altar-lamps were lighted, –
   An old marsh-donkey came,
Bold as a guest invited,
   And stared at the guttering flame.

The storm beat on at the windows,
   The water splashed on the floor,
And a wet, yoke-weary bullock
   Pushed in through the open door.

'How do I know what is greatest,
How do I know what is least?
That is my Father's business,'
Said Eddi, Wilfrid's priest.

'But – three are gathered together –
Listen to me and attend.
I bring good news, my brethren!'
Said Eddi, of Manhood End.

And he told the Ox of a manger,
And a stall in Bethlehem,
And he spoke to the Ass of a Rider
That rode to Jerusalem.

They steamed and dripped in the chancel,
They listened and never stirred,
While, just as though they were Bishops,
Eddi preached them The Word.

Till the gale blew off on the marshes
And the windows showed the day,
And the Ox and the Ass together
Wheeled and clattered away.

And when the Saxons mocked him,
Said Eddi of Manhood End,
'I dare not shut His chapel
On such as care to attend.'

Rudyard Kipling

For the Children or the Grown-ups?

'Tis the week before Christmas and every night
    As soon as the children are snuggled up tight
And have sleepily murmured their wishes and prayers,
    Such fun as goes on in the parlour downstairs!
For Father, Big Brother, and Grandfather too,
    Start in with great vigour their youth to renew.
The grown-ups are having great fun – all is well;
    And they play till it's long past their hour for bed.

They try to solve puzzles and each one enjoys
    The magical thrill of mechanical toys,
Even Mother must play with a doll that can talk,
    And if you assist it, it's able to walk.
It's really no matter if paint may be scratched,
    Or a cogwheel, a nut, or a bolt gets detached;
The grown-ups are having great fun – all is well;
    The children don't know it, and Santa won't tell.

Unknown

My Christmas : Mum's Christmas

decorations	climbing up to the loft on a wobbly ladder, probably falling.
a Christmas tree	pine needles and tinsel all over the carpet.
lots of food	preparations and loads of dishes to be washed.
crackers	crumpled paper everywhere.
presents	money down the drain.
sweets	indigestion and tooth-ache.
parties	late nights, and driving back through the dark.
snow to play in	getting soaked and frozen whenever outside.

Sarah Forsyth

Christmas is really for the Children

Christmas is really
for the children.
Especially for children
who like animals, stables,
stars and babies wrapped
in swaddling clothes.
Then there are wise men,
kings in fine robes,
humble shepherds and a
hint of rich perfume.

Easter is not really
for the children
unless accompanied by a
cream filled egg.
It has whips, blood, nails,
a spear and allegations
of body snatching.
It involves politics, God
and the sins of the world.
It is not good for people
of a nervous disposition.
They would do better to
think on rabbits, chickens
and the first snowdrop
of spring.
Or they'd do better to
wait for a re-run of
Christmas without asking
too many questions about
what Jesus did when he grew up
or whether there's any connection.

Steve Turner

Hang up the Baby's Stocking!

Hang up the baby's stocking!
Be sure you don't forget! The
dear little dimpled darling, she
never saw Christmas yet! But
I've told her all about it, and
she opened her big blue eyes;
and I'm sure she understood
it– she looked so funny and
wise. ∵ Dear, what a tiny
stocking! It doesn't take much
to hold such little pink toes
as baby's away from the frost
and cold. But then, for the
baby's Christmas, it will
never do at all. Why! Santa
wouldn't be looking for any-
thing half so small.
    ∵ I know what will do for
    the baby. I've thought of
    the very best plan. I'll borrow
    a stocking of Grandma's
    the longest that ever I can.
    And you'll hang it by mine,
    dear mother, right here in
    the corner, so! And leave
    a letter to Santa, and
    fasten it on to the toe.
        ∴ Write – this is the
        baby's stocking that hangs
        in the corner here. You never have
        seen her, Santa, for she only came this
        year. But she's just the blessed'st baby.
        And now before you go, just cram her
        stocking with goodies, from the top
        clean down to the toe!

Unknown

A Visit from St Nicholas

'Twas the night before Christmas, when all through the house
Not a creature was stirring, not even a mouse;
The stockings were hung by the chimney with care,
In hopes that St Nicholas soon would be there;
The children were nestled all snug in their beds,
While visions of sugar-plums danced in their heads;
And mamma in her 'kerchief, and I in my cap,
Had just settled our brains for a long winter's nap,
When out on the lawn there arose such a clatter,
I sprang from the bed to see what was the matter.
Away to the window I flew like a flash,
Tore open the shutters and threw up the sash.
The moon on the breast of the new-fallen snow
Gave the lustre of mid-day to objects below,
When, what to my wondering eyes should appear,
But a miniature sleigh, and eight tiny reindeer,
With a little old driver, so lively and quick,
I knew in a moment it must be St Nick.
More rapid than eagles his coursers they came,
And he whistled, and shouted, and called them by name;
'Now Dasher! now, Dancer! now, Prancer and Vixen!
On, Comet! on, Cupid! on, Donner and Blitzen!
To the top of the porch! to the top of the wall!
Now dash away! dash away! dash away all!'
As dry leaves that before the wild hurricane fly,
When they meet with an obstacle, mount to the sky,
So up to the house-top the coursers they flew,
With the sleigh full of toys, and St Nicholas too.
And then, in a twinkling, I heard on the roof
The prancing and pawing of each little hoof.
As I drew in my head, and was turning around,
Down the chimney St Nicholas came with a bound.
He was dressed all in fur, from his head to his foot,
And his clothes were all tarnished with ashes and soot.
A bundle of toys he had flung on his back,
And he looked like a pedlar, just opening his pack.
His eyes – how they twinkled! his dimples how merry!
His cheeks were like roses, his nose like a cherry!

His droll little mouth was drawn up like a bow,
And the beard of his chin was as white as the snow;
The stump of a pipe he held tight in his teeth,
And the smoke it encircled his head like a wreath;
He had a broad face and a little round belly,
That shook when he laughed, like a bowlful of jelly.
He was chubby and plump, a right jolly old elf,
And I laughed when I saw him, in spite of myself;
A wink of his eye and a twist of his head,
Soon gave me to know I had nothing to dread.
He spoke not a word, but went straight to his work,
And filled all the stockings; then turned with a jerk,
And laying his finger aside of his nose,
And giving a nod, up the chimney he rose;
He sprang to his sleigh, to his team gave a whistle,
And away they all flew like the down of a thistle.
But I heard him exclaim, 'ere he drove out of sight,
'Happy Christmas to all, and to all a good-night.'

Clement Clark Moore

little tree
little silent Christmas tree
you are so little
you are more like a flower

who found you in the green forest
and were you very sorry to come away?
see   i will comfort you
because you smell so sweetly

i will kiss your cool bark
and hug you safe and tight
just as your mother would,
only don't be afraid

look   the spangles
that sleep all the year in a dark box
dreaming of being taken out and allowed to shine,
the balls the chains red and gold the fluffy threads,

put up your little arms
and i'll give them all to you to hold
every finger shall have its ring
and there won't be a single place dark or unhappy

then when you're quite dressed
you'll stand in the window for everyone to see
and how they'll stare!
oh but you'll be very proud

and my little sister and i will take hands
and looking up at our beautiful tree
we'll dance and sing
'Noel Noel'

e. e. cummings

The Christmas Tree

Outside the world was full, plural,
Plants and beasts ran and roared.

You could say the tree is standing still
And dead quiet, brought indoors alone.
For an hour the cat waited for it to move.
His murderous face is off guard now.

The cat is a scrounger from the farm.
They do not feed him. He has to hunt.
'That's what they'm for.'

Tonight we work at the tree like dressmakers,
In the breeze of its faint healthy smell.

Light will be rounded up and festooned over it.
That's what it's for.

It shall not be burnt.
At Epiphany we will try re-planting it.
It may go yellow while we still hope
And while the spring goes green.

Perhaps it will look down on the thatch yet.

Patricia Beer

Christmas Tree

Star over all
Eye of the night
Stand on my tree
Magical sight
Green under frost
Green under snow
Green under tinsel
Glitter and glow
Appled with baubles
Silver and gold
Spangled with fire
Warm over cold.

Laurence Smith

Christmas Tree

Stores and filling stations prefer a roof
For Christmas trees, away from pilfering children,
And set the cost against their income tax;
Florists sell them at something a foot
And like the rest of Christmas illuminations
They use electricity in off-peak periods:
Enough to make you steal an honest tree
From a Forestry Commission planting.
Isn't there somewhere in the woods a fir
Beneath whose natural pagoda of branches
Deer bivouac, that dredges silver
From an accident of moonlight
And roofs the moss from snow that falls on higher ground?
Isn't there the child, beneath the presents
We heap upon him, that we are fond of?

Stanley Cook

Advice from Poor Robin's Almanack

Now that the time has come wherein
Our Saviour Christ was born,
The larder's full of beef and pork,
The granary's full of corn,
As God hath plenty to thee sent,
Take comfort of thy labours,
And let it never thee repent
To feed thy needy neighbours.

Keeping Christmas

How will you your Christmas keep?
Feasting, fasting, or asleep?
Will you laugh or will you pray,
Or will you forget the day?

Be it kept with joy or pray'r,
Keep of either some to spare;
Whatsoever brings the day,
Do not keep but give away.

Eleanor Farjeon

The Reminder

While I watch the Christmas blaze
Paint the room with ruddy rays,
Something makes my vision glide
To the frosty scene outside.

There, to reach a rotting berry,
Toils a thrush – constrained to very
Dregs of food by sharp distress,
Taking such with thankfulness.

Why, O starving bird, when I
One day's joy would justify,
And put misery out of view,
Do you make me notice you?

Thomas Hardy

Christmas: 1924

'Peace upon earth!' was said. We sing it,
And pay a million priests to bring it.
After two thousand years of mass
We've got as far as poison-gas.

Thomas Hardy

Now every man at my request
Be glad and merry all in this fest.

Lett no man cum into this hall,
Grome, page, nor yet marshall,
But that sum sport he bryng withall;
For now is the time of Cristymas!

If he say he can nowght do,
Then for my love aske hym no mo,
But to the stokkis then lett hym go,
For now is the time of Cristymas!

December

Glad Christmas comes, and every hearth
   Makes room to give him welcome now,
E'en want will dry its tears in mirth,
   And crown him with a holly bough;
Though tramping 'neath a winter sky,
   O'er snowy paths and rimy stiles,
The housewife sets her spinning by
   To bid him welcome with her smiles.

Each house is swept the day before,
   And windows stuck with evergreens,
The snow is besom'd from the door,
   And comfort crowns the cottage scenes.
Gilt holly, with its thorny pricks,
   And yew and box, with berries small,
These deck the unused candlesticks,
   And pictures hanging by the wall.

Neighbours resume their annual cheer,
   Wishing, with smiles and spirits high,
Glad Christmas and a happy year
   To every morning passer-by;
Milkmaids their Christmas journeys go,
   Accompanied with favour'd swain;
And children pace the crumping snow,
   To taste their granny's cake again.

The shepherd, now no more afraid,
   Since custom doth the chance bestow,
Starts up to kiss the giggling maid
   Beneath the branch of misletoe
That 'neath each cottage beam is seen,
   With pearl-like berries shining gay;
The shadow still of what hath been,
   Which fashion yearly fades away.

John Clare

Christmas Card

You have anti-freeze in the car, yes,
   But the shivering stars wade deeper.
Your scarf's tucked in under your buttons,
   But a dry snow ticks through the stubble.
Your knee-boots gleam in the fashion,
   But the moon must stay

      And stamp and cry
      As the holly the holly
      Hots its reds

Electric blanket to comfort your bedtime
   The river no longer feels its stones.
Your windows are steamed by dumpling laughter
   The snowplough's buried on the drifted moor.
Carols shake your television
   And nothing moves on the road but the wind

      Hither and thither
      The wind and three
      Starving sheep.

Redwings from Norway rattle at the clouds
  But comfortless sneezers puddle in pubs.
The robin looks in at the kitchen window
  But all care huddles to hearths and kettles.
The sun lobs one wet-snowball feebly
  Grim and blue

     The dusk of the coombe
     And the swamp woodland
     Sinks with the wren.

See old lips go purple and old brows go paler.
  The stiff crow drops in the midnight silence.
Sneezes grow coughs and coughs grow painful.
  The vixen yells in the midnight garden.
You wake with the shakes and watch your breathing
  Smoke in the moonlight – silent, silent.

     Your anklebone
     And your anklebone
     Lie big in the bed.

Ted Hughes

Ghost Story

Bring out the tall tales now that we told
by the fire as the gaslight bubbled like a diver.
Ghosts whooed like owls in the long nights
when I dared not look over my shoulder; animals
lurked in the cubbyhole under the stairs where the
gas meter ticked. And I remember that we went
singing carols once, when there wasn't the shaving
of a moon to light the flying streets. At the end
of a long road was a drive that led to a large
house, and we stumbled up the darkness of the drive
that night, each one of us afraid, each one holding
a stone in his hand in case, and all of us too brave
to say a word. The wind through the trees
made noises as of old and unpleasant and maybe
webfooted men wheezing in caves. We reached
the black bulk of the house.
'What shall we give them? Hark the Herald?'
'No,' Jack said, 'Good King Wenceslas.
I'll count three.'
One, two, three, and we began to sing,
our voices high and seemingly distant in the
snow–felted darkness around the house that
was occupied by nobody we knew. We stood
close together, near the dark door.
'*Good King Wenceslas looked out*
On the Feast of Stephen . . .'
And then a small, dry voice, like the voice
of someone who has not spoken for a long time,
joined our singing: a small dry eggshell voice
from the other side of the door: a small dry voice
through the keyhole. And when we stopped running
we were outside *our* house; the front room was lovely:
balloons floated under the hot-water-bottle-gulping gas;
everything was good again and shone over the town.

'Perhaps it was a ghost,' Jim said.
'Perhaps it was trolls,' Dan said,
who was always reading.

'Let's go in and see if there's any jelly left,'
Jack said. And we did that.

Dylan Thomas

Christmas Eve

The roofs over the shops
Are grey and quiet already.
In two hours from now
Light and noise will drain
From counter and cash desk
Into the streets and away.

People will go home
To windows that all year
Turned into their rooms
But goggle outwards now
With lit-up trees.

Tinsel wriggles in the heating.
Everything hangs.

As it gets dark a drunk
Comes tacking up the road
In a white macintosh
Charming as a yacht.

Patricia Beer

Reindeer Report

Chimneys: colder.
Flightpaths: busier.
Driver: Christmas (F)
Still baffled by postcodes.

Children: more
And stay up later.
Presents: heavier.
Pay: frozen.

Mission in spite
Of all this
Accomplished.

U. A. Fanthorpe

Christmas Night

On the wind, a drifting echo
of simple songs. In the city
the streetlamps, haloed innocents,
click into instant sleep.
The darkness at last breathes.

In dreams of wholeness, irony
is a train melting to distance;
and the word, a delighted child
gazing in safety at
a star solid as flesh.

Lawrence Sail

Sretan Božić   Nollarg shonna

Rõõmsaid
Jõulu Pühi   Mutlu Noeller   Glaedelig Jul

Felices Pascuas y Próspero
Año Nuevo

Srećan Božić i Hristos se rodi   Feliz Navidad

Nadolig Llawen   Gajan Kristnaskon

Priecigus Ziemsvetkus

Fröhliche Weihnachten

Buon Natale   Vrolyk kerstfeest
en Gelukkig
Nieuw Jaar

Hauskaa
Joulua   Joyeux Noël

Boas   Boas Festas e Feliz Ano Novo
Festas

God Jul og Godt   Khrystos
Kellemes   Rodywsiq
Karácsonyi
Nyttår   ünnepeket   God Jul

Geseënde Kersfees

108

Merry Christmas

Good Will to Men – Christmas Greetings in Six Languages

At Christmas, when old friends are meeting,
We give that long-loved joyous greeting –
    'Merry Christmas!'

While hanging sheaves for winter birds
Friends in Norway call the words,
    'God Jul!'

With wooden shoes ranged on the hearth,
Dutch celebrators cry their mirth,
    'Vrolyk Kerstfeest!'

In France, that land of courtesy,
Our welcome to our guests would be,
    'Joyeux Noël!'

Enshrining Christmas in her art,
Italy cries from a full heart,
    'Buon Natale!'

When in the land of Christmas trees,
Old Germany, use words like these –
    'Fröhliche Weihnachten!'

Though each land names a different name,
Good will rings through each wish the same –
    'Merry Christmas!'

Dorothy Brown Thompson

Christmas Bells

I heard the bells on Christmas day
Their old familiar carols play,
   And wild and sweet
   The words repeat
Of 'Peace on earth, good will to men!'

And thought how, as the day had come,
The belfries of all Christendom
   Had rolled along
   The unbroken song,
Of 'Peace on earth, good will to men!'

Till ringing, singing on its way,
The world revolved from night to day –
   A voice, a chime
   A chant sublime,
Of 'Peace on earth, good will to men!'

And in despair I bowed my head;
'There is no peace on earth,' I said,
   'For hate is strong
   And mocks the song
Of peace on earth, good will to men!'

Then pealed the bells more loud and deep:
'God is not dead; nor doth he sleep!
   The wrong shall fail,
   The right prevail,
With peace on earth, good will to men!'

Henry Wadsworth Longfellow

Christmas Day

Nature's decorations glisten
   Far above their usual trim;
Birds on box and laurels listen
   As so near the cherubs hymn.

Boreas now no longer winters
   On the desolated coast;
Oaks no more are riv'n in splinters
   By the whirlwind and his host.

Spinks and ouzles sing sublimely,
   'We too have a Saviour born,'
Whiter blossoms burst untimely
   On the blest Mosaic thorn.

God all-bounteous, all-creative,
   Whom no ills from good dissuade,
Is incarnate, and a native
   Of the very world he made.

Christopher Smart

The Burning Babe

As I in hoary winter's night stood shivering in the snow,
Surprised I was with sudden heat which made my heart to glow;
And lifting up a fearful eye to view what fire was near,
A pretty Babe all burning bright did in the air appear;
Who scorchèd with excessive heat, such floods of tears did shed,
As though his floods should quench his flames which with his tears were
    fed.

'Alas!' quoth he, 'but newly born in fiery heats I fry,
Yet none approach to warm their hearts or feel my fire but I.
My faultless breast the furnace is, the fuel wounding thorns;
Love is the fire, and sighs the smoke, the ashes shame and scorns;
The fuel justice layeth on, and mercy blows the coals;
The metal in this furnace wrought are men's defilèd souls:
For which, as now on fire I am to work them to their good,
So will I melt into a bath to wash them in my blood.'
With this he vanished out of sight and swiftly shrunk away,
And straight I callèd unto mind that it was Christmas day.

Robert Southwell

Men may talk of Country-Christmasses

Men may talk of country-Christmasses and court-gluttony,
Their thirty-pound buttered eggs, their pies of carps' tongues,
Their pheasants drenched with ambergris, the carcases
Of three fat wethers bruised for gravy, to
Make sauce for a single peacock; yet their feasts
Were fasts, compared with the city's . . .

Did you not observe it?
There were three sucking pigs served up in a dish,
Ta'en from the sow as soon as farrowèd,
A fortnight fed with dates, and muskadine,
That stood my master in twenty marks apiece,
Besides the puddings in their bellies, made
Of I know not what. – I dare swear the cook that dressed it
Was the devil, disguised like a Dutchman.

Philip Massinger

A Dish for a Poet

Take a large olive, stone it and then stuff it with a paste made of anchovy, capers, and oil.

Put the olive inside a trussed and boned bec–figue.

Put the bec–figue inside a fat ortolan.

Put the ortolan inside a boned lark.

Put the stuffed lark inside a boned thrush.

Put the thrush inside a fat quail.

Put the quail, wrapped in vine-leaves, inside a boned lapwing.

Put the lapwing inside a boned golden plover.

Put the plover inside a fat, boned, red-legged partridge.

Put the partridge inside a young, boned, and well-hung woodcock.

Put the woodcock, rolled in bread-crumbs, inside a boned teal.

Put the teal inside a boned guinea-fowl.

Put the guinea-fowl, well larded, inside a young and boned tame duck.

Put the duck inside a boned and fat fowl.

Put the fowl inside a well-hung pheasant.

Put the pheasant inside a boned and fat wild goose.

Put the goose inside a fine turkey.

Put the turkey inside a boned bustard.

Having arranged your roast after this fashion, place it in a large saucepan with onions stuffed with cloves, carrots, small squares of ham, celery, mignonette, several strips of bacon well-seasoned, pepper, salt, spice, coriander seeds, and two cloves of garlic.

Seal the saucepan hermetically by closing it with pastry. Then put it for ten hours over a gentle fire, and arrange it so that the heat can penetrate evenly. An oven moderately heated will suit better than the hearth.

Before serving, remove the pastry, put the roast on a hot dish after having removed the grease – if there is any – , and serve.

Traditional, c. 1814

Christmas Dinner

We were all sitting round the table.
There was roast turkey
there were roast potatoes
there were roast parsnips
there were broccoli tips
there was a dishful of crispy bacon off the turkey
there was wine, cider, lemonade
and milk for the youngsters.
Everything was set.
It was all on the table.
We were ready to begin.
Suddenly there was a terrible terrible scream.
Right next to the turkey was a worm.
A dirty little worm wriggling about like mad.

For a moment everyone looked at it.
Someone said very quietly, 'Oh dear.'
And everyone was thinking things like –
'How did it get there?'
'If that came out of the turkey,
I don't want any of it.'
or
'I'm not eating any Christmas dinner. It could be full of
dirty little wriggly worms.'

Now – as it happens,
I don't mind wriggly worms.
There was plenty of room for it
at the table.
It was just that . . . that . . .
no-one had asked it to come over
for Christmas dinner.

So I said,
'I don't think it came out of the turkey. I think –
It came off the bottom of the milk bottle.'
And I picked up the worm,
and put it out the door to spend Christmas day
in a lovely patch of wet mud.
Much nicer place to be –
for a worm.

Michael Rosen

The Fire

The fire, with well-dried logs supplied,
Went roaring up the chimney wide;
The huge hall-table's oaken face,
Scrubb'd till it shone, the day to grace,
Bore then upon its massive board
No mark to part the squire and lord.
Then was brought in the lusty brawn,
By old blue-coated serving-man;
Then the grim boar's head frown'd on high,
Crested with bays and rosemary.
Well can the green-garb'd ranger tell,
How, when, and where, the monster fell;
What dogs before his death he tore,
And all the baiting of the boar.
The wassel round, in good brown bowls
Garnish'd with ribbons, blithely trowls.
There the huge sirloin reek'd; hard by
Plum-porridge stood, and Christmas pie;
Nor fail'd old Scotland to produce,
At such high tide, her savoury goose.

Walter Scott

In the Workhouse

It is Christmas Day in the Workhouse,
  And the cold bare walls are bright
With garlands of green and holly,
  And the place is a pleasant sight:
For with clean-washed hands and faces,
  In a long and hungry line
The paupers sit at the tables,
  For this is the hour they dine.

And the guardians and their ladies,
  Although the wind is east,
Have come in their furs and wrappers,
  To watch their charges feast;
To smile and be condescending,
  Put pudding on pauper plates,
To be hosts at the workhouse banquet
  They've paid for – with the rates.

Oh, the paupers are meek and lowly
  With their 'Thank'ee kindly, mum's';
So long as they fill their stomachs,
  What matter it whence it comes?
But one of the old men mutters,
  And pushes his plate aside:
'Great God!' he cries; 'but it chokes me!
  For this is the day *she* died.'

The guardians gazed in horror,
  The master's face went white;
'Did a pauper refuse their pudding?'
  'Could their ears believe aright?'
Then the ladies clutched their husbands,
  Thinking the man would die,
Struck by a bolt, or something,
  By the outraged One on high.

But the pauper sat for a moment,
  Then rose 'mid a silence grim,
For the others had ceased to chatter,
  And trembled in every limb.
He looked at the guardians' ladies,
  Then, eyeing their lords, he said,
'I eat not the food of villains
  Whose hands are foul and red:

'Whose victims cry for vengeance
    From their dank, unhallowed graves.'
'He's drunk!' said the workhouse master.
    'Or else he's mad, and raves.'
'Not drunk, or mad,' cried the pauper,
    'But only a hunted beast,
Who, torn by the hounds and mangled,
    Declines the vulture's feast.

'I care not a curse for the guardians,
    And I won't be dragged away.
Just let me have the fit out,
    It's only on Christmas Day
That the black past comes to goad me,
    And prey on my burning brain;
I'll tell you the rest in a whisper, –
    I swear I won't shout again.

'Keep your hands off me, curse you!
    Hear me right out to the end.
You come here to see how the paupers
    The season of Christmas spend.
You come here to watch us feeding,
    As they watch the captured beast.
Hear why a penniless pauper
    Spits on your paltry feast.

'Do you think I will take your bounty,
    And let you smile and think
You're doing a noble action
    With the parish's meat and drink?
Where is my wife, you traitors –
    The poor old wife you slew?
Yes, by the God above us,
    My Nance was killed by you!

'Last winter my wife lay dying,
  Starved in a filthy den;
I had never been to the parish, –
  I came to the parish then.
I swallowed my pride in coming,
  For, ere the ruin came,
I held up my head as a trader,
  And I bore a spotless name.

'I came to the parish, craving
  Bread for a starving wife,
Bread for the woman who'd loved me
  Through fifty years of life;
And what do you think they told me,
  Mocking my awful grief?
That "the House" was open to us,
  But they wouldn't give "out relief".

'I slunk to the filthy alley –
  'Twas a cold, raw Christmas eve –
And the bakers' shops were open,
  Tempting a man to thieve;
But I clenched my fists together,
  Holding my head awry,
So I came to her empty-handed,
  And mournfully told her why.

 Then I told her "the House" was open;
  She had heard of the ways of *that*,
For her bloodless cheeks went crimson,
  And up in her rags she sat,
Crying, "Bide the Christmas here, John,
  We've never had one apart;
I think I can bear the hunger, –
  The other would break my heart."

'All through that eve I watched her,
   Holding her hand in mine,
Praying the Lord, and weeping
   Till my lips were salt as brine.
I asked her once if she hungered,
   And as she answered "No,"
The moon shone in at the window
   Set in a wreath of snow.

'Then the room was bathed in glory,
   And I saw in my darling's eyes
The far-away look of wonder
   That comes when the spirit flies;
And her lips were parched and parted,
   And her reason came and went,
For she raved of our home in Devon,
   Where our happiest years were spent.

'And the accents, long forgotten,
   Came back to the tongue once more,
For she talked like the country lassie
   I woo'd by the Devon shore.
Then she rose to her feet and trembled,
   And fell on the rags and moaned,
And, "Give me a crust – I'm famished –
   For the love of God!" she groaned.

'I rushed from the room like a madman,
   And flew to the workhouse gate,
Crying, "Food for a dying woman!"
   And the answer came, "Too late."
They drove me away with curses;
   Then I fought with a dog in the street,
And tore from the mongrel's clutches
   A crust he was trying to eat.

'Back, through the filthy by-lanes!
    Back, through the trampled slush!
Up to the crazy garret,
    Wrapped in an awful hush.
My heart sank down at the threshold,
    And I paused with a sudden thrill,
For there in the silv'ry moonlight
    My Nance lay, cold and still.

'Up to the blackened ceiling
    The sunken eyes were cast –
I knew on those lips all bloodless
    My name had been the last;
She'd called for her absent husband –
    O God! had I but known! –
Had called in vain, and in anguish
    Had died in that den – *alone.*

'Yes, there, in a land of plenty,
    Lay a loving woman dead,
Cruelly starved and murdered
    For a loaf of the parish bread.
At yonder gate, last Christmas,
    I craved for a human life.
You, who would feast us paupers,
    What of my murdered wife!

'There, get ye gone to your dinners;
    Don't mind me in the least;
Think of the happy paupers
    Eating your Christmas feast;
And when you recount their blessings
    In your smug parochial way,
Say what you did for *me*, too,
    Only last Christmas Day.'

George R. Sims

A Summer Christmas in Australia

The Christmas dinner was at two,
And all that wealth or pains could do
Was done to make it a success;
And marks of female tastefulness,
And traces of a lady's care,
Were noticeable everywhere.
The port was old, the champagne dry,
And every kind of luxury
Which Melbourne could supply was there.
They had the staple Christmas fare,
Roast beef and turkey (this was wild),
Mince-pies, plum-pudding, rich and mild,
One for the ladies, one designed
For Mr. Forte's severer mind,
Were on the board, yet in a way
It did not seem like Christmas day
With no gigantic beech yule-logs
Blazing between the brass fire-dogs,
And with 100° in the shade
On the thermometer displayed.
Nor were there Christmas offerings
Of tasteful inexpensive things,
Like those which one in England sends
At Christmas to his kin and friends,
Though the Professor with him took
A present of a recent book
For Lil and Madge and Mrs. Forte,
And though a card of some new sort
Had been arranged by Lil to face
At breakfast everybody's place.
When dinner ended nearly all
Stole off to lounges in the hall.
All save the two old folks and Lil,
Who made their hearts expand and thrill
By playing snatches, slow and clear,
Of carols they'd been used to hear
Some half a century ago

At High Wick Manor, when the two
Were bashful maidens: they talked on,
Of England and what they had done
On bygone Christmas nights at home,
Of friends beyond the Northern foam,
And friends beyond that other sea,
Yet further – whither ceaselessly
Travellers follow the old track,
But whence no messenger comes back.

Douglas Sladen

African Christmas

Here are no signs of festival,
No holly and no mistletoe,
No robin and no crackling fire,
And no soft, feathery fall of snow.

In England one could read the words
Telling how shepherds in the fold
Followed the star and reached the barn
Which kept the Saviour from the cold.

And picture in one's mind the scene –
The tipsy, cheerful foreign troops,
The kindly villagers who stood
About the Child in awkward groups.

But in this blazing Christmas heat
The ox, the ass, the bed of hay
The shepherds and the Holy Child
Are stilted figures in a play.

Exiles, we see that we, like slaves
To symbol and to memory,
Have worshipped, not the incarnate Christ,
But tinsel on the Christmas tree.

John Press

Pilgrims in Mexico

'Who knocks at my door, so late in the night?'
'We are pilgrims, without shelter, and we want only a place to rest.'
'Go somewhere else and disturb me not again.'
'But the night is very cold. We have come from afar, and we are very
    tired.'
'But who are you? I know you not.'
'I am Joseph of Nazareth, a carpenter, and with me is Mary, my wife,
    who will be the mother of the Son of God.'
'Then come into my humble home, and welcome! And may the Lord
    give shelter to my soul when I leave this world!'

Traditional

Roman Presents

Because, this month, when napkins, pretty spoons,
Papers, wax tapers and tall jars of prunes
Fly to and fro, I've sent you nothing but books,
My humble, home-made verses, I may seem
Stingy or impolite. But I abhor
The tricks of the angler's trade. Gifts are like hooks,
And flies, as everyone knows, fool greedy bream.
So, Quintianus, when a man who's poor
Sends nothing to a rich friend, it's an act
Of generosity – in point of tact.

Martial
Translated by James Michie

Christmas 1970

A little girl called Silé Javotte
Said 'Look at the lovely presents I've got'
While a little girl in Biafra said
'Oh what a lovely slice of bread'.

Spike Milligan

Christmas

The bells of waiting Advent ring,
   The Tortoise stove is lit again
And lamp-oil light across the night
   Has caught the streaks of winter rain
In many a stained-glass window sheen
From Crimson Lake to Hooker's Green.

The holly in the windy hedge
   And round the Manor House the yew
Will soon be stripped to deck the ledge,
   The altar, font and arch and pew,
So that the villagers can say
'The church looks nice' on Christmas Day.

Provincial public houses blaze
   And Corporation tramcars clang,
On lighted tenements I gaze
   Where paper decorations hang,
And bunting in the red Town Hall
Says 'Merry Christmas to you all.'

And London shops on Christmas Eve
   Are strung with silver bells and flowers
As hurrying clerks the City leave
   To pigeon-haunted classic towers,
And marbled clouds go scudding by
The many-steepled London sky.

And girls in slacks remember Dad,
   And oafish louts remember Mum,
And sleepless children's hearts are glad,
   And Christmas-morning bells say 'Come!'
Even to shining ones who dwell
Safe in the Dorchester Hotel.

And is it true? And is it true,
   This most tremendous tale of all,
Seen in a stained-glass window's hue,
   A Baby in an ox's stall?
The Maker of the stars and sea
Become a Child on earth for me?

And is it true? For if it is,
   No loving fingers tying strings
Around those tissued fripperies,
   The sweet and silly Christmas things,
Bath salts and inexpensive scent
And hideous tie so kindly meant,

No love that in a family dwells,
   No carolling in frosty air,
Nor all the steeple-shaking bells
   Can with this simple truth compare –
That God was Man in Palestine
And lives today in Bread and Wine.

John Betjeman

A Child's Christmas Day

He opens his eyes with a cry of delight,
There's a toy-shop all round him, a wonderful sight!
The fairies have certainly called in the night.

They are quiet at first – both the girls and the boys,
Too happy to make any riot or noise,
And they mutually show to each other their toys.

Then Uncle appears with a smile on his lips,
As his fingers deep down in his pocket he dips,
A performance which ends in a series of 'tips'.

Next Sally brings Pudding – the spirit burns blue,
They all dance around her, a merry young crew,
For they hope to eat mince-pie and plum-pudding too.

But, see! In the nursery a terrible racket,
The dolls lose their heads, there are rents in each jacket,
And if you've a toy, it's the fashion to crack it.

The floor is all littered with signs of the fray,
He is sulky and tired with much eating and play,
And Nurse too is cross as she bears him away.

Unknown

Afterthought

For weeks before it comes I feel excited, yet when it
At last arrives, things all go wrong:
My thoughts don't seem to fit.

I've planned what I'll give everyone and what they'll give to me,
And then on Christmas morning all
The presents seem to be

Useless and tarnished. I have dreamt that everything would come
To life – presents and people too.
Instead of that, I'm dumb,

And people say, 'How horrid! What a sulky little boy!'
And they are right. I *can't* seem pleased.
The lovely shining toy

I wanted so much when I saw it in a magazine
Seems pointless now. And Christmas too
No longer seems to mean

The hush, the star, the baby, people being kind again.
The bells are rung, sledges are drawn,
And peace on earth for men.

Elizabeth Jennings

Christmas Day

Small girls on trikes
Bigger on bikes
Collars on tykes

Looking like cads
Patterned in plaids
Scarf-wearing dads

Chewing a choc
Mum in a frock
Watches the clock

Knocking in pans
Fetching of grans
Gathering of clans

Hissing from tins
Sherries and gins
Upping of chins

Corks making pops
'Just a few drops'
Watering of chops

All this odd joy
Tears at a broken toy
Just for the birth long ago of a boy

Roy Fuller

Grandmother Jackson

She spent three hundred and sixty four days a year
owning eighty-five bedrooms in her sea-front hotel,
many glass cabinets of untouched bone china,
and the black silk dress
she sat correct in, every Christmas morning.

The one morning of her year
she gave up for her grandchildren;
interrogating us, giving us long,
cool stares through steel frames,
as we shifted gawkily in Sunday Best.

We went with half fear, half longing
for the moments after her inspection;
the hunt for giant packages beneath the tree,
'Not to be opened until after the Queen's speech.'

A train set played with twice.
The huge doll's broken eyes
down in the cellar. Faint memories
checked the full cartwheel of our joy
as we lolloped back along the beach.

David Jackson

Christmas Thank You's

Dear Auntie
Oh, what a nice jumper
I've always adored powder blue
and fancy you thinking of
orange and pink
for the stripes
how clever of you!

Dear Uncle
The soap is
terrific
So
useful
and such a kind thought and
how did you guess that
I'd just used the last of
the soap that last Christmas brought

Dear Gran
Many thanks for the hankies
Now I really can't wait for the flu
and the daisies embroidered
in red round the 'M'
for Michael
how
thoughtful of you!

Dear Cousin
What socks!
and the same sort you wear
so you must be
the last word in style
and I'm certain you're right that the
luminous green
will make me stand out a mile

Dear Sister
I quite understand your concern
it's a risk sending jam in the post
But I think I've pulled out
all the big bits
of glass
so it won't taste too sharp
spread on toast

Dear Grandad
Don't fret
I'm delighted
So *don't* think your gift will
offend
I'm not at all hurt
that you gave up this year
and just sent me
a fiver
to spend

Mick Gowar

A Roman Thank-you Letter

For New Year, Postumus, ten years ago,
You sent me four pounds of good silver-plate.
The next year, hoping for a rise in weight
(For gifts should either stay the same or grow),
I got two pounds. The third and fourth produced
Inferior presents, and the fifth year's weighed
Only a pound – Septicius' work, ill-made
Into the bargain. Next I was reduced
To an eight-ounce oblong salad-platter; soon
It was a miniature cup that tipped the scales
At even less. A tiny two-ounce spoon
Was the eighth year's surprise. The ninth, at length,
And grudgingly, disgorged a pick for snails
Lighter than a needle. Now, I note, the tenth
Has come and gone with nothing in its train.
I miss the old four pounds. Let's start again!

Martial
Translated by James Michie

Christmas Bills

See dear Pater with the bills –
    Christmas bills!
What unhappy omination their presence
    now fulfils!
How they wrinkle, wrinkle, wrinkle
    Pater's frowning brow!
While figures oversprinkle
Paper that seems to twinkle
    Three columns in a row.
Keeping time, time, time
In a sort of Runic rhyme
To the concatenacious thought that so
    uncomfortably fills
Pater's mind from the bills, bills, bills,
  Bills, bills bills –
From the winking and the blinking of the bills.

Here are Monsieur Vintner's bills,
  Sherry bills!
How the Spanish golden liquor woeful
  melancholy kills!
In the murky air of night
What glories, what delight!
  From the molten golden stream
  Like a happy summer dream;
    And all the time
  What a fragrant sweet perfume
  Floats all about the room
    Above the table.
  Oh! how the bosom thrills!
But how it saddens with the bills –
  Christmas bills,
  Vintner's bills,
And all the other ills
That the time is bringing in
  With the bills, bills, bill, bills,
    Bills, bills, bills –
That the time is bringing in with the bills.

Joseph Hatton

Christmas

What, do they suppose that everything has been said that *can* be said about any one Christmas thing?

About beef, for instance?
About mince-pie?
About ivy?
About mistletoe?
About hunt-the-slipper?
About blind-man's buff?
About thread-the-needle?

About puss-in-the-corner?
About forfeits?
About the bell-man?
About chilblains?
About the fire?
About school-boys?
About Christmas boxes?
About Hogmany?
About mumming?
About brown?
About hoppy-horse?
About wakes?
About hackin?
About going-a-gooding?

About plum-pudding?
About holly?
About rosemary?
About Christmas Eve?
About hot cockles?
About shoeing-the-wild-mare?
About he-can-do-little-that-can't-do-this?
About snap-dragon?
About Miss Smith?
About the waits?
About carols?
About the clock on it?
About their mothers?
About turkeys?
About goose-pie?
About saluting the apple-trees?
About plum-porridge?
About hoppings?
About 'feed-the-dove'?
About Yule-dough?
About loaf-stealing?

About Julklaps? (who has exhausted the subject, we should like to know?)

About elder-wine?
About cards?
About gifts?
About Twelfth-cake?
About characters?
About aldermen?
About all being in the wrong?
About all being in the right?

About wad-shooting?
About pantomime?
About New-Year's Day?
About wassail?
About king and queen?
About eating too much?
About the doctor?
About charity?
About faith, hope and endeavour?

About the greatest plum-pudding for the greatest number?

Leigh Hunt

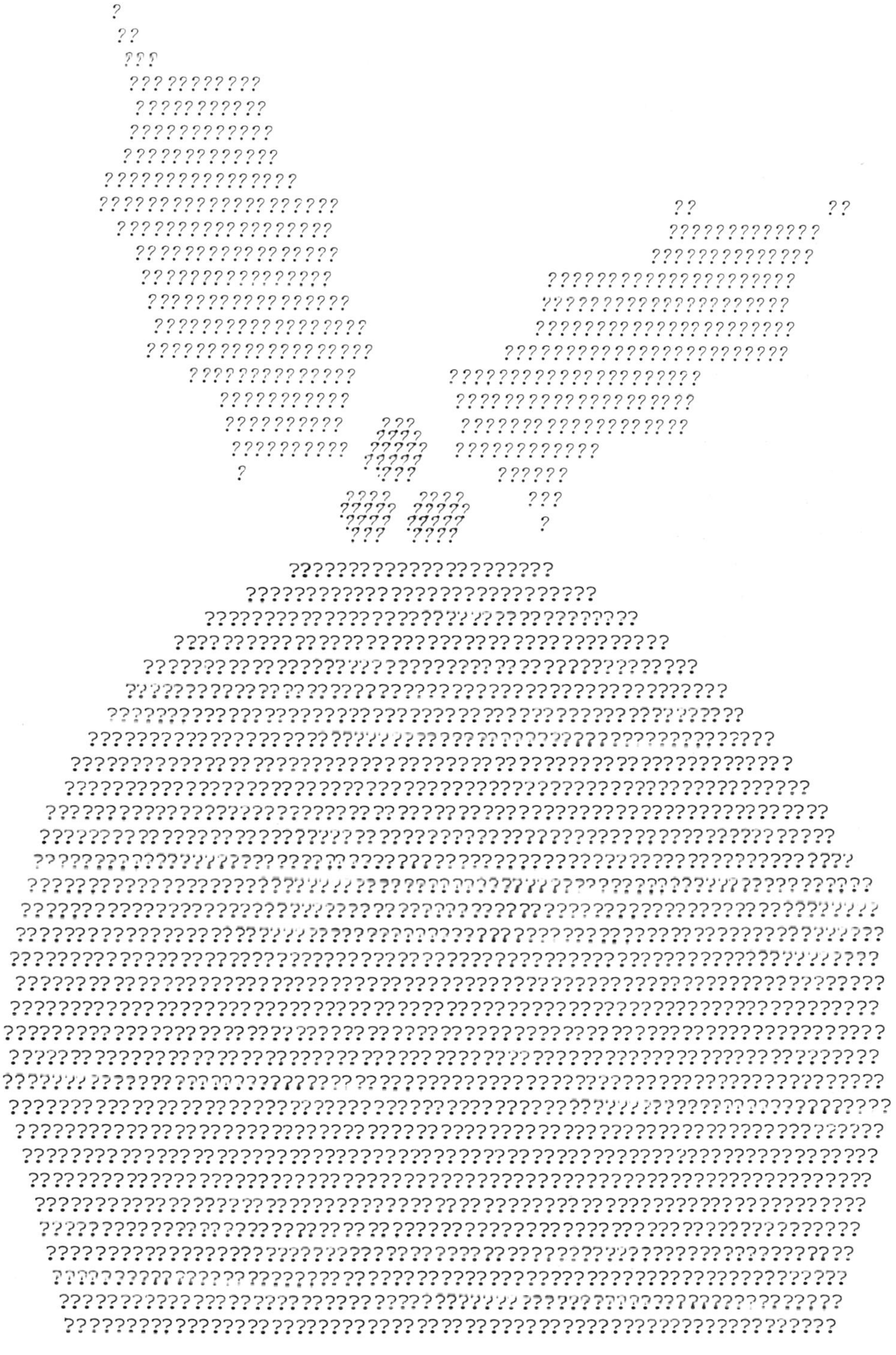

After Christmas

Darkness begins a
retreat: the cold light flows back
over the dead land.

Put the tree out now:
hang nuts on its branches – see feathered
decorations come.

Take down the Christmas
cards: arrowheads in the dust
point to spring cleaning.

Pull down the paper
chains: the room grows tall, the floor
deep in coloured snow.

Cold bites deep: warm your
mind at Christmas memories
and look for snowdrops.

Michael Richards

Open you the East door
And let the New Year in.

Well, so that is that

Well, so that is that. Now we must dismantle the tree,
Putting the decorations back into their cardboard boxes –
Some have got broken – and carrying them up into the attic.
The holly and the mistletoe must be taken down and burnt,
And the children got ready for school. These are enough
Left overs to do, warmed-up, for the rest of the week –
Not that we have much appetite, having drunk such a lot,
Stayed up so late, attempted – quite unsuccessfully –
To love all of our relatives, and in general
Grossly overestimated our powers. Once again
As in previous years we have seen the actual Vision and failed
To do more than entertain it as an agreeable
Possibility. Once again we have sent Him away,
Begging though to remain His disobedient servant,
The promising child who cannot keep His word for long.
The Christmas Feast is already a fading memory,
And already the mind begins to be vaguely aware
Of an unpleasant whiff of apprehension at the thought
Of Lent and Good Friday which cannot, after all, now
Be very far off. But, for the time being, here we all are,
Back in the moderate Aristotelian city
Of darning and the Eight-Fifteen, where Euclid's geometry
And Newton's mechanics would account for our experience,
And the kitchen table exists because I scrub it.
It seems to have shrunk during the holidays. The streets
Are much narrower than we remembered; we had forgotten
The office was as depressing as this. To those who have seen
The Child, however dimly, however incredulously
The Time Being is, in a sense, the most trying time of all.
For the innocent children who whispered so excitedly
Outside the locked door where they knew the presents to be
Grew up when it opened. Now, recollecting that moment
We can repress the joy, but the guilt remains conscious;
Remembering the stable where for once in our lives
Everything became a You and nothing was an It.
And craving the sensation but ignoring the cause,
We look round for something, no matter what, to inhibit
Our self-reflection, and the obvious thing for that purpose
Would be some great suffering. So, once we have met the Son,

We are tempted ever after to pray to the Father:
'Lead us not into temptation and evil for our sake'.
They will come all right, don't worry; probably in a form
That we do not expect, and certainly with a force
More dreadful than we can imagine. In the meantime
There are bills to be paid, machines to keep in repair,
Irregular verbs to learn, the Time Being to redeem
From insignificance. The happy morning is over,
The night of agony still to come; the time is noon:
When the Spirit must practise his scales of rejoicing
Without even a hostile audience, and the Soul endure
A silence that is neither for nor against her faith
That God's Will will be done, that, in spite of her prayers,
God will cheat no one, not even the world of its triumph.

W. H. Auden

The Old Year

The Old Year's gone away
   To nothingness and night:
We cannot find him all the day
   Nor hear him in the night:
He left no footstep, mark or place
   In either shade or sun:
The last year he'd a neighbour's face,
   In this he's known by none.

All nothing everywhere:
   Mists we on mornings see
Have more of substance when they're here
   And more of form than he.
He was a friend by every fire,
   In every cot and hall –
A guest to every heart's desire,
   And now he's nought at all.

Old papers thrown away,
   Old garments cast aside,
The talk of yesterday,
   All things identified;
But times once torn away
   No voices can recall:
The eve of New Year's Day
   Left the Old Year lost to all.

John Clare

The New Year

Here we bring new water
　　From the well so clear,
For to worship God with,
　　This happy New Year.
Sing levy-dew, sing levy-dew,
　　The water and the wine;
The seven bright gold wires
　　And the bugles they do shine.

Sing reign of Fair Maid,
　　With gold upon her toe –
Open you the West Door,
　　And turn the Old Year go:
Sing reign of Fair Maid,
　　With gold upon her chin –
Open you the East Door,
　　And let the New Year in.

Unknown

New Year Song

Now there comes
  The Christmas rose
    But that is eerie
          too like a ghost
    Too like a creature
          preserved under glass
    A blind white fish
          from an underground lake
    Too like last year's widow
          at a window
             And the worst cold's to come.

Now there comes
  The tight-vest lamb
    With its wriggle eel tail
          and its wintry eye
    With its ice-age mammoth
          unconcern
    Letting the aeon
          seconds go by
    With its little peg hooves
          to dot the snow
    Following its mother
          into worse cold and worse
             And the worst cold's to come.

Now there come
  The weak-neck snowdrops
    Bouncing like fountains
          and they stop you, they make you
    Take a deep breath
          make your heart shake you
    Such a too much of a gift
          for such a mean time
    Nobody knows
          how to accept them
    All you can do
          is gaze at them baffled
             And the worst cold's to come.

And now there comes
  The brittle crocus
    To be nibbled by the starving hares
               to be broken by snow
    Now comes the aconite
             purpled by cold
    A song comes into
             the storm-cock's fancy
    And the robin and the wren
             they rejoice like each other
    In an hour of sunlight
             for something important
                 Though the worst cold's to come.

Ted Hughes

January

The snow has melted now,
Uncovered on the lawn
The holly that we threw
Out when the year was done.
The crimson berries glow
Brilliant against the green,
And on a sculptured bough
Hard, black as ebony,
A robin-redbreast flings
Into the winter sky
His little sparks of song
Like promises of Spring.

Douglas Gibson

January

Under a white coverlet of snow
The infant year is lying,
A leaden canopy of cloud above.
Now to this cradle haste
The royal seasons, in their robes,
Of green, crimson, and rich russet,
Bearing their gifts – the sunshine gold of spring,
Incense of summer flowers, and acrid tang
Of autumn's burning leaves.

John Heath-Stubbs

February

Splish splosh, February-fill-the-dike,
Sleet in the wind, mud underfoot.
What hint, you ask, of spring? But trust
The honest mistle-thrush, who shouts his song
And builds his nest – a less accomplished singer
Than is the clear-voiced mavis, but he is brave and true.

And trust the aconite and crocus, bright
As wicks of thread which now are lighted up
For ceremonials of Candlemas.

John Heath-Stubbs

Ceremony upon Candlemas Eve

Down with the rosemary, and so
Down with the bays and mistletoe;
Down with the holly, ivy, all
Wherewith ye dressed the Christmas hall;
That so the superstitious find
No one least branch there left behind;
For look, how many leaves there be
Neglected there, maids, trust to me,
So many goblins you shall see.

Robert Herrick

At Candlemas

'If Candlemas be fine and clear
There'll be two winters in that year';

But all the day the drumming sun
Brazened it out that spring had come,

And the tall elder on the scene
Unfolded the first leaves of green.

But when another morning came
With frost, as Candlemas with flame,

The sky was steel, there was no sun,
The elder leaves were dead and gone.

Out of a cold and crusted eye
The stiff pond stared up at the sky,

And on the scarcely breathing earth
A killing wind fell from the north;

But still within the elder tree
The strong sap rose, though none could see.

Charles Causley

Winter Cricket

A cricket on a rubbish-tip
Fiddles a winter tune;
He has no heating problems,
Scraps enough and to spare.

Robin in the holly
And the wren in the ivy-tod
Fluff up their plumes, and try to keep warm
With a tootle on their pipes –
Waiting for spring to come.

And spring will come.

John Heath-Stubbs

Snowdrops

The first day of this month I saw
Their active spearheads. Dry and raw

They rose from grass, beside my pond,
In a white stockade. And now, beyond

Far evergreens, more gather, and
Advance on dead ground. Dour they stand,

As if numb earth depended on
Their stolid hold. And what has gone,

Or will go, when they give, means time.
Time to be emptying ponds of slime,

Time to be slow, time to work hard.
I see them thicken, yard by yard.

These are the first of our strong flowers.
Before the spring, or April showers,

They teem with loyalty, and fight
For a place in the sun. Static in flight

Their icy lances pierce with green
Last year's downed leaves. I touch one. Clean

And moist upon my reaching palm,
I feel its energy, its calm.

George MacBeth

The Fight of the Year

'And there goes the bell for the third month
and Winter comes out of its corner looking groggy
Spring leads with a left to the head
followed by a sharp right to the body
   daffodils
   primroses
   crocuses
   snowdrops
   lilacs
   violets
   pussywillow
Winter can't take much more punishment
and Spring shows no signs of tiring
   tadpoles
   squirrels
   baalambs
   badgers
   bunny rabbits
   mad march hares
   horses and hounds
Spring is merciless

Winter won't go the full twelve rounds
    bobtail clouds
    scallywaggy winds
    the sun
    a pavement artist
    in every town
A left to the chin
and Winter's down!
    1 tomatoes
    2 radish
    3 cucumber
    4 onions
    5 beetroot
    6 celery
    7 and any
    8 amount
    9 of lettuce
    10 for dinner
Winter's out for the count
Spring is the winner!'

Roger McGough

Index of Titles and First Lines

Acknowledgements

The editors and publishers gratefully acknowledge permission to reproduce the following copyright material:

W. H. Auden: 'The Flight Into Egypt', Part III, from "For the Time Being" ('Well, so that is that'), copyright 1944 by W. H. Auden from *W. H. Auden: Collected Poems*, edited by Edward Mendelson. Reprinted by permission of Faber & Faber Ltd., and Random House, Inc. Patricia Beer: 'The Christmas Tree' and 'Christmas Eve' from *Selected Poems*, copyright © P. Beer 1980. Reprinted by permission of the Hutchinson Publishing Group Ltd. John Betjeman: 'Advent 1955' from *Uncollected Poems*; 'Christmas' from *Collected Poems*. Reprinted by permission of John Murray (Publishers) Ltd. Charles Causley: 'Mary's Song' and 'Angels' Song' from *The Gift of a Lamb* (Robson Books); 'On the thirteenth day of Christmas'; 'Innocent's Song'; 'Sailor's Carol' and 'At Candlemas' from *Collected Poems* (Macmillan). Reprinted by permission of David Higham Associates Ltd. G. K. Chesterton: 'A Christmas Carol' from *Collected Poems*. Reprinted by permission of A. P. Watt Ltd., on behalf of the Estate of the late G. K. Chesterton. Elizabeth Coatsworth: 'The Barn' from *Compass Rose*, copyright 1929 by Coward, McCann, Inc., © renewed 1957 by Elizabeth Coatsworth. Reprinted by permission of Putnam Publishing Group. Stanley Cook: 'Christmas Tree', first published in *Poems for Christmas* (Harry Chambers/Peterloo Poets, 1981). Reprinted by permission of the author. E. E. Cummings: 'little tree' published in the UK in *E. E. Cummings: Complete Poems 1913–1962* and in the US in *Tulips and Chimneys*, copyright 1923, 1925 and renewed 1951, 1953 by E. E. Cummings, copyright © 1973, 1976 by the Trustees for the E. E. Cummings Trust, copyright © 1973, 1976 by George James Firmage. Reprinted by permission of Granada Publishing Ltd., and Liveright Publishing Corporation. Walter de la Mare: 'A Ballad of Christmas'. Reprinted by permission of The Literary Trustees of Walter de la Mare and The Society of Authors as their representative. Patric Dickinson: 'Advent; A Carol' and 'St. Stephen's Day' from *The Bearing Beast* (Chatto & Windus 1976). Reprinted by permission of the author. Gwen Dunn: 'Journey Back to Christmas'. Reprinted by permission of the author. T. S. Eliot: 'The Journey of the Magi' from *Collected Poems 1909–1962*, copyright 1936 by Harcourt Brace Jovanovich, Inc., copyright © 1963, 1964 by T. S. Eliot. Reprinted by permission of Faber & Faber Ltd., and Harcourt, Brace Jovanovich, Inc. U. A. Fanthorpe: 'Reindeer Report', 'B.C.: A.D.' and 'What the Donkey Saw' first published in *Poems for Christmas* (Harry Chambers/Peterloo Poets, 1981). Reprinted by permission of the author. Eleanor Farjeon: 'Keeping Christmas' from *Silver-Sand and Snow* (Michael Joseph). Reprinted by permission of David Higham Associates Ltd. Robert Finch: 'The Crib' from *Christmas in Canada* (J. M. Dent & Sons, Canada, Ltd.). Sarah Forsyth: 'My Christmas: Mum's Christmas' from *A Child's View of Christmas* (1980). Reprinted by permission of Exley Publications Ltd. Peter Freuchen: 'The Mother's Song' from "Distant Voices" from *Book of the Eskimos*. Reprinted by permission of George Weidenfeld & Nicolson Ltd. Roy Fuller: 'Christmas Day' from *Upright Downfall*. Reprinted by permission of the author. Douglas Gibson: 'January'. Reprinted by permission of the author. Mick Gowar: 'Christmas Thank-you's' from *Swings and Roundabouts*. Reprinted by permission of Collins Publishers. Robert Graves: 'Carol of Patience' from *Collected Poems*. Reprinted by permission of A. P. Watt Ltd., on the author's behalf. Josef Hanzlik: 'Clap Your Hands for Herod' (Potlesk pro Herodesa), copyright © Josef Hanzlik 1967. Reprinted by permission of Dilia, Literary Agency, Czechoslovakia. John Heath-Stubbs: 'Winter Cricket', 'January', 'February' and 'December' from "Poems for a Calendar" from *Naming the Beasts* (Carcanet). Reprinted by permission of David Higham Associates Ltd. Heinrich Heine: 'The Wise Men Ask the Children the Way' from the German of Heinrich Heine, translated by Geoffrey Grigson in *The Cherry Tree*. Reprinted by permission of Geoffrey Grigson. Miroslav Holub: 'How to paint a perfect Christmas' from Miroslav Holub: *Selected Poems*, translated by Ian Milner and George Theiner (Penguin Modern European Poets 1967) pp. 59–61. Copyright © Miroslav Holub, 1967; Translation copyright © Penguin Books 1967. Reprinted by permission of Penguin Books Ltd. Ted Hughes: 'Christmas Card' and 'New Year Song' from *Season Songs*. Text copyright © 1973 by Ted Hughes. 'Minstrel's Song' from "The Coming of the Kings" published in the UK in *The Coming of the Kings and other Plays* and in the US in *The Tiger's Bones and Other Plays for Children*. Text copyright © 1974 by Ted Hughes. Reprinted by permission of Faber & Faber Ltd., and Viking Penguin, Inc. David Jackson: 'Grandmother

Jackson'. Reprinted by permission of the author.   Elizabeth Jennings: 'Afterthought' from *The Secret Brother* (Macmillan). Reprinted by permission of David Higham Associates Ltd. Rudyard Kipling: 'Eddi's Service', copyright 1910 by Rudyard Kipling from *Rudyard Kipling's Verse: Definitive Edition*. Reprinted by permission of A. P. Watt Ltd., The National Trust and Doubleday and Company, Inc.   Laurie Lee: 'Christmas Landscape' from *The Bloom of Candles*. Reprinted by permission of the author.   Madeleine L'Engle: 'O Simplicitas' from *The Weather of the Heart*, copyright © Crosswicks, 1978. Reprinted by permission of Harold Shaw Publishers.   Robert Lowell: 'The Holy Innocents' published in the UK in *Poems 1938–49* and in the US in *Lord Weary's Castle*, copyright 1946, 1974 by Robert Lowell. Reprinted by permission of Faber & Faber Ltd., and Harcourt Brace Jovanovich, Inc.   George MacBeth: 'Snowdrops' from *Poems From Oby* (Secker & Warburg). Reprinted by permission of the author.   Norman MacCaig: 'Sleet' from *Measures*. Reprinted by permission of Chatto & Windus Ltd.   Roger McGough: 'The Fight of the Year' from *Watchwords*. Reprinted by permission of Jonathan Cape Ltd., and A. D. Peters & Co., Ltd.   Louis MacNeice: 'Christmas Shopping' from *Collected Poems*. Reprinted by permission of David Higham Associates Ltd. Martial: Epigrams 18 and 71 from *Martial's Epigrams*, translated by James Michie (Penguin). Reprinted by permission of the translator.   Spike Milligan: 'Christmas 1970' from *Small Dreams of a Scorpion*. Reprinted by permission of Michael Joseph Ltd.   Kevin Nichols: 'The Feast of Stephen' from *A Partridge in a Pear Tree* (ed. Braybrooke; Darton, Longman & Todd Ltd.).   Norman Nicholson: 'Carol' from *Five Rivers* (Faber). Reprinted by permission of the author and David Higham Associates Ltd. 'The Shepherds' Carol' and 'Carol for the last Christmas Eve'. Reprinted by permission of the author.   Leslie Norris: 'Mice in the Hay', 'The Shepherd's Dog' and 'Camels of the Kings'. Reprinted by permission of the author.   Gareth Owen: 'Winter Days' from *Salford Road* (Kestrel Books 1979) p. 65, copyright © 1971, 1974, 1976, 1979 by Gareth Owen. Reprinted by permission of Penguin Books Ltd.   Christopher Pilling: 'The Adoration of the Magi' first published in *Poems for Christmas* (Harry Chambers/Peterloo Poets 1981). Reprinted by permission of the author.   John Press: 'African Christmas' from *Uncertainties*. Reprinted by permission of the author.   W. R. Rodgers: 'Carol' from *Europa and the Bull*. Reprinted by permission of Secker & Warburg Ltd.   Theodore Roethke: 'The Coming of the Cold', copyright 1941 by Theodore Roethke, from *The Collected Poems of Theodore Roethke*. Reprinted by permission of Faber & Faber Ltd., and Doubleday & Company, Inc.   Michael Rosen: 'Christmas Dinner'. Reprinted by permission of the author.   Lawrence Sail: 'Christmas Night' first published in *Poems for Christmas* (Harry Chambers/Peterloo Poets 1981). Reprinted by permission of the author.   Clive Sansom: 'Snowflakes' from *An English Year* (Chatto); 'The Inn-keeper's Wife' from *The Witnesses* (Methuen). Reprinted by permission of David Higham Associates Ltd.   Peter Scupham: 'Twelfth Night' from *Summer Palaces*, copyright © Peter Scupham 1980. Reprinted by permission of Oxford University Press.   Dylan Thomas: 'Ghost Story' from *Quite Early One Morning* (Dent). Reprinted by permission of David Higham Associates Ltd.   Steve Turner: 'Christmas is Really for the Children' from *Up To Date*. Reprinted by permission of the author and Hodder & Stoughton Ltd.   James Walker: 'Safe' from *Tapestry* (ed. Eric Williams, Edward Arnold 1974).   Richard Wilbur: 'A Christmas Hymn' from *Advice to a Prophet and Other Poems*, copyright © 1961 by Richard Wilbur. Reprinted by permission of Faber & Faber Ltd., and Harcourt Brace Jovanovich, Inc.   Charles Williams: 'Kings Came Riding' from *Modern Verse for Little Children* (OUP). Reprinted by permission of David Higham Associates Ltd.   Andrew Young: 'Christmas Day' from *Complete Poems*. Reprinted by permission of Secker & Warburg Ltd.

While every effort has been made to secure permission, we may have failed in a few cases to trace or contact the copyright holder. We apologize for any apparent negligence.

We should also like to thank the following artists for providing the illustrations:

Peter Bailey *(72-74 and 102/103)*,   Ian Beck *(114/115)*,   Alan Cracknall *(69)*,   Allan Curless *(57 and 70/71)*,   Kevin Dean *(144/145)*,   Sarah De'Ath *(52)*,   Bob Dewar *(132/133)*,   Cathie Felstead *(20/21 and 128/129)*,   Hannah Firmin *(25 and 112/113)*,   Lynette Hemmant *(78–82)*,   Tudor Humphries *(19 and 30/31)*,   Charles Keeping *(118–123)*,   Priscilla Lamont *(94)*,   Jane Lydbury *(10/11)*,   Tony Morris *(36–41 and 59)*,   Paddy Mounter *(117, 135 and 154/155)*,   David Parkins *(44, 45, 51, 87, 105, 106/107, 137, 143, 150 and 152/153)*,   Abigail Pizer *(130/131)*,   Geoff Taylor *(60/61)*,   Martin White *(9,14/15, 46/47, 48/49, 62, 67, 88/89, 96/97, 110, 111, 124/125, 126 and 147)*,   John Wilkinson *(141)*,   Ann Winterbotham *(100)*,   Freire Wright *(84/85 and 148/149)*,   and Kathy Wyatt *(32/33)*, Cover illustration by Jane Ray

We wish you all a very happy and peaceful Christmas.